PROHIBITION BAKERY

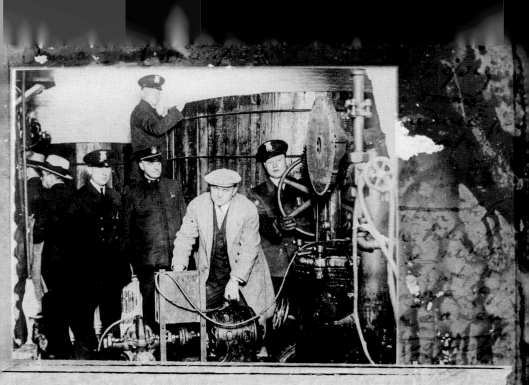

PROHIBITION BAKERY

LESLIE FEINBERG

BROOKE SIEM

EAST VILLAGE

TATTOO

PROHIBITION BAKERY

STERLING EPICURE
New York

STERLING EPICURE
New York

An Imprint of Sterling Publishing
1166 Avenue of the Americas
New York, NY 10036

STERLING EPICURE is a trademark of Sterling Publishing Co., Inc.
The distinctive Sterling logo is a registered trademark of Sterling Publishing Co., Inc.

Text © 2015 by Leslie Feinberg and Brooke Siem
Principal photography © 2015 by Sterling Publishing Co., Inc.

Cover design and art direction by Jo Obarowski
Interior design by Amy Trombat

Principal photography by Bill Milne with the following additions:
© akg-images 25 left; Courtesy Leslie Feinberg and Brooke Siem 310, 311; © David Goddard
Photography 312 & 313 portraits; Instagram @prohibitionbakery 4, 5, 14 right, 19, 22 left & center,
23 top, 24 center & right, 25 right, 26, 27, 29, 32, 34, 37, 39, 43, 62 bottom, 77, 126 bottom,
138 bottom, 145, 223, 312 & 313 background; Library of Congress 2, 22 right, 69, 72, 81,
95, 104 top, 107, 111, 118, 126 top, 129, 138 top, 212 top, 215, 246 top, 271, 283;
National Archives 3 top, 153; © Siem Photography 11, 62 top; Amy Trombat 294;
Courtesy Wikimedia Foundation/Orange County Archives 179, 249

ISBN 978-1-4549-1696-3

Distributed in Canada by Sterling Publishing
c/o Canadian Manda Group, 664 Annette Street
Toronto, Ontario, Canada M6S 2C8
Distributed in the United Kingdom by GMC Distribution Services
Castle Place, 166 High Street, Lewes, East Sussex, England BN7 1XU
Distributed in Australia by Capricorn Link (Australia) Pty. Ltd.
P.O. Box 704, Windsor, NSW 2756, Australia

For information about custom editions, special sales, and premium and corporate
purchases, please contact Sterling Special Sales at 800-805-5489 or
specialsales@sterlingpublishing.com.

Manufactured in Canada

2 4 6 8 10 9 7 5 3 1

www.sterlingpublishing.com

To our dads, who would have gotten the biggest kick out of this.

Lower East Side

New York City

▼

INTRODUCTION

This is not just the story of Prohibition Bakery. While we would like to consider ourselves interesting enough to fill volumes with witty anecdotes and appropriate hyperbole, a quick look at our day-to-day lives indicates that we are simply a duo who stumbled into entrepreneurship and have yet to sell to Facebook for $18 billion. In fact, Prohibition Bakery was an accident. Brooke was killing time as an underemployed former chef, and Leslie was bartending after being laid off in the great Publishing Purge of 2008. We both wanted something different, and after a fateful GChat conversation in 2011, we found a new direction:

> Brooke: We can get drunk while baking to take the edge off.
> Leslie: It's like you read my mind. I like the boozin',
> and I loves the bakin'.
> Brooke: I'm actually quite serious. Screw chocolate and
> vanilla cupcakes.
> Leslie: I know. I'm serious too. Guinness cupcakes, please.
> Death to Red Velvet!

As you can see, there was no logical discussion, no plan, no question of how to take this zygote of an idea and make it work—Prohibition Bakery just suddenly existed. We would figure out the rest later, and really, we're still figuring it out.

On any given day we have to answer dozens of questions, from which tequila to use in a new cupcake to how to grow our crazy idea from a 220-square-foot bakery into the next cupcake empire.

And yet, every day people ask us for advice on an array of topics. Luckily we cover

different areas of expertise. Any concerns about cocktails, cookie baking, classic comedy, the art of pretending like you give a shit, or the long-term prospects of that girl you've been kind of dating should be directed toward Leslie. Any technical questions about cooking, lifting heavy things, obscure New York State business laws, and strategy for exorcising a demon dog should be directed toward Brooke. In this book we will only cover liquor and baking. Perhaps, if enough people buy our humble cookbook, instead of borrowing it from a friend or downloading it from Kickass Torrents, we'll write a companion book on the specifics of terrible first dates and canine exorcism. But for now, we'll stick to our bread and butter—or rather, cupcakes and buttercream.

All of the recipes in this book have been adapted for the home baker and use ingredients and tools that should be (somewhat) familiar and easy to source. Meaning: The recipes in this book are not exactly the recipes we use at Prohibition Bakery, and thus you should not expect them to taste exactly the same. What sort of businesspeople would we be if we freely gave our recipes to the world? It would be as if Apple started selling a make-your-own iPhone kit for $39.99. However, we've created 55 original recipes just for you, which means you have 55 opportunities to impress your friends or your mother-in-law.

Measurements are defined first by volume (cups and teaspoons/tablespoons) and then by weight (grams)—for your own good, damn it. Trust us,

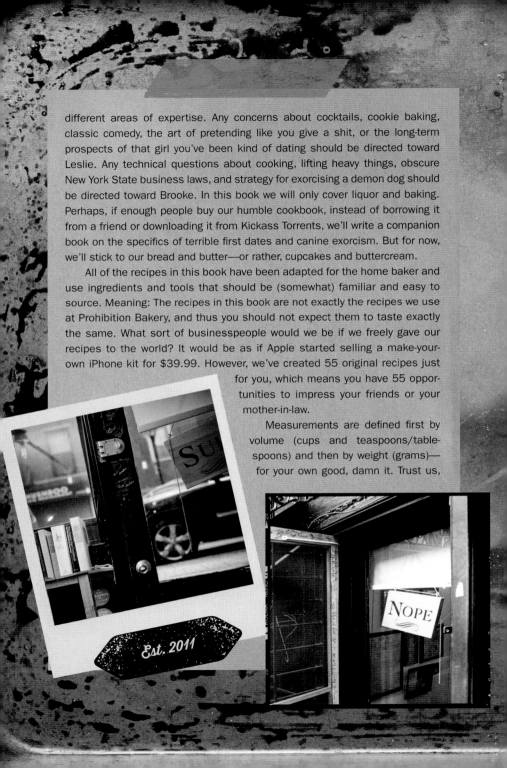

it's worth investing in a kitchen scale. You'll have more consistent results and way less room for error if you weigh all of your ingredients. And, you'll look like a super cool chef. And if it all goes to hell, well you'll have plenty of booze around to numb your shame and disappointment.

By buying this book, you have acknowledged a desire to create something, and that is fantastic because (a) we want your money and/or to write another book, and (b) feeding those you love is one of the oldest expressions of affection there is. Ever since Crog brought the first woolly mammoth back to the cave and made sure his Cro-Magnon lady got that choice rump piece, people have been using food as a way to convey love, respect, and/or a desire to impress those around them. Yes, you could have gone out and bought a box of cupcakes from the gas station (they even come with a free Big Gulp and plastic footballs stuck into the creepy Styrofoam-like frosting!), but you didn't, and for that you should feel very proud. Once you've mastered the techniques and recipes in this book, you'll be able to start turning your favorite cocktails into cupcakes.

Now, get to baking. It accidentally changed our lives, so who knows what will happen with you. If our humble book somehow alters the course of your existence, email us at info@prohibition bakery.com, or send a handmade thank-you card to our storefront at 9 Clinton Street, New York, NY 10002, to let us know. Drawings, puns, and gift cards are encouraged. Please, no glitter. ▲

Lulu + Brooke

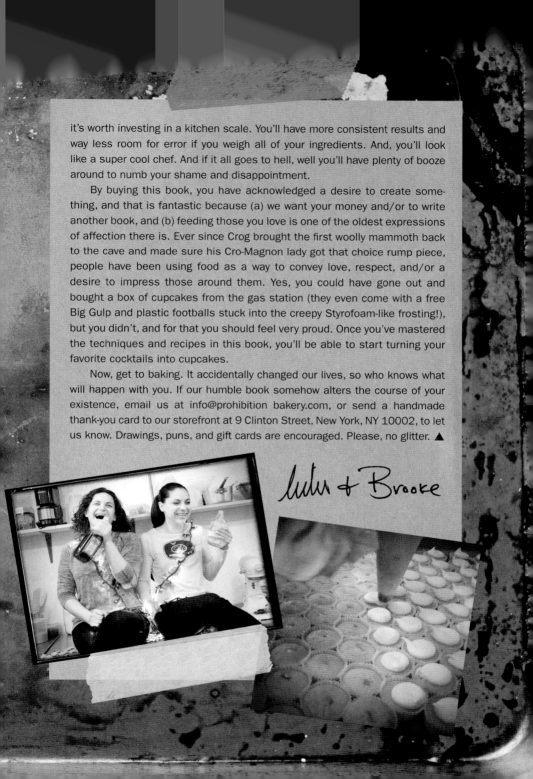

Building a Kitchen

IF YOU'VE MADE IT THIS FAR, YOU'RE CLEARLY ATTEMPTING TO EXPAND YOUR CULINARY MIND AND BAKE OUTSIDE THE BOX MIX. WHILE BAKING ACCURATELY CERTAINLY DEMANDS SOME SPECIFIC TOOLS, IT DOES NOT REQUIRE ALL THE BRIGHTLY BRANDED GADGETS THAT CELEBRITY CHEFS AND INFOMERCIALS CLAIM YOU NEED. IN FACT, IF YOU WALK INTO ANY RESTAURANT KITCHEN, YOU'LL MOST LIKELY ENCOUNTER AN ARRAY OF BANGED-UP POTS AND PANS, LADLES, AND STRAINERS THAT MAY OR MAY NOT STILL BE THEIR ORIGINAL SHAPE. SO, INSTEAD OF SPENDING YOUR MONEY ON THE LATEST BRIGHT ORANGE NONSTICK POT WITH A RUBBERIZED MATCHING HANDLE AND A MATCHING LID THAT WILL LIKELY NOT HEAT EVENLY, TAKE THAT MONEY AND BUY YOURSELF A KITCHEN SCALE AND A DIGITAL THERMOMETER. YOU'RE WELCOME.

$\bigtriangledown$

TOOLS AND APPLIANCES

(that we need to talk you into buying)

▶ **Bowls** *(not the one you smoke out of)*—Plastic and Pyrex bowls don't do much in the way of conducting heat, so their use is limited. Invest in some all-metal bowls of varying sizes.

▶ **Digital/instant read candy thermometer**—Next to a kitchen scale, a digital thermometer is one of the most important cooking and baking tools, especially for a novice. Look for one with a clip to attach to the side of the pot—you'll save yourself a lot of burned fingertips trying to retrieve dropped thermometers drowned in hot caramel sauce.

▶ **Heat-proof rubber spatulas**—Your average rubber spatula is not designed to withstand heat. Unless you want melted plastic in your cooking, go ahead and get a heat-proof spatula.

▶ **Kitchen blowtorch**—If you're anything like us, you've been waiting for an excuse to buy a blowtorch. Just in case you need convincing, a blowtorch is the best way to toast meringues and brûlée crèmes. Plus you can make indoor s'mores, evenly roast peppers, or crisp the top of mac 'n' cheese.

▶ **Kitchen scale**—If you learn just one thing from our cookbook, let it be this: a kitchen scale is the most useful tool in all of baking. While the book lists ingredients in traditional cups and ounces, any good baker will tell you that weighing ingredients in grams is the way to go. Weighing all your ingredients in grams guarantees accuracy, whereas one person's cup of flour can vary wildly from another's. Kitchen scales can be heavily marked up in retail, so during your search, look for postal scales that max out around 5,000 grams.

- **Mini cupcake liners**—Mini cupcakes require mini liners. We shouldn't have to explain this concept.

- **Mini cupcake tins**—Every cupcake recipe in this book is designed to be presented as a mini cupcake. Can you make a full-sized cupcake out of these recipes? Theoretically, yes, but we don't recommend it. Our cupcakes are designed to be enjoyed in one bite, which means that the frosting, filling, cake, and garnishes all mingle together to create an amazing taste experience. If you try to bake a bigger cupcake, the ratios of filling to frosting to cake will immediately be thrown off. So, take our advice and invest in a mini cupcake tin. If you don't, don't be cranky when things don't turn out correctly.

- **Piping bag/tips**—While you're welcome to frost all your boozy cupcakes with a spoon or knife, your friends will be way more impressed if you learn how to pipe frosting. Whether you prefer disposable or reusable bags is up to you, but the only way to get perfect swirled frosting is to invest in a set of pastry tips.

- **Squeeze bottles**—Squeeze bottles will instantly improve the quality of your baking life. Use large bottles to neatly squeeze cupcake batter into liners, and use small bottles to fill each cupcake with filling. If you go against our advice and try to do this with spoons and piping bags, think of us fondly when you're taking an extra 45 minutes to clean up the mess you made.

- **Oven thermometer**—Our recipes say to bake at 325°F, but all ovens are different, so you may need to adjust the temperature. Once you find a happy place, oven thermometers will guarantee accuracy for each bake.

► **Stand mixer**—The stand mixer is one of the easiest kitchen appliances to talk yourself out of. It may seem unnecessary if you already have a hand mixer, but its benefits are so great that we encourage you to make the investment. In addition to their ability to beat, whisk, and knead, stand mixers allow you to work hands-free, which is perhaps their most underappreciated value. We use standard-issue, 4-gallon stand mixers for everything we do at the bakery. Take it from us, this will be more than enough. You can go crazy and buy something bigger and fancier, but it's a waste of money and counter space. We bought a 10-gallon mixer when we first opened, and we've used the damn thing maybe five times. Meanwhile, we've lost 4 square feet of counter space. When your bakery (or kitchen) is only 220 square feet, that's a big loss. Hand mixers will do the trick for many mixing tasks but they seriously cut down on your multitasking ability and will likely end in a batter-splattered kitchen.

TOOLS AND APPLIANCES*

(that your mom probably already bought for you)

▶ **Chef's chopping knife** (a good one)

▶ **Coffee grinder** (great for grinding spices and nuts)

▶ **Cutting board**

▶ **Hand grater/microplane grater**

▶ **Liquid measuring cup**

▶ **Measuring spoons**

▶ **Mesh strainer**

▶ **Saucepans** (aka regular old pots), medium and large

▶ **Sheet pans** (aka cookie sheets)

---

*We promise that this is all you really need, and that any kitchen gadget beyond the items listed above is simply an extra bonus. Of course, if you want to buy us the personalized hot dog warmer or the mechanical swirling spaghetti spork found on page 95 of the SkyMall catalogue, our address is 9 Clinton Street, New York, NY 10002. Danke.

THINGS YOU SHOULD ALWAYS HAVE ON HAND

- ▶ **Baking powder**
- ▶ **Baking soda**
- ▶ **Butter**, unsalted
- ▶ **Chocolate**, bittersweet
- ▶ **Chocolate**, milk
- ▶ **Cream of tartar**
- ▶ **Eggs**, large and cage/antibiotic-free
- ▶ **Flour**, all-purpose
- ▶ **Heavy cream**
- ▶ **Olive oil**
- ▶ **Salt** (kosher)
- ▶ **Shortening**, vegetable-based*
- ▶ **Sour cream**, full fat
- ▶ **Sugar**, confectioners' (aka powdered or 10×)
- ▶ **Sugar**, granulated
- ▶ **Sugar**, light brown
- ▶ **Yogurt**, full or 2 percent fat

---

*See page 29 that talks about high-ratio shortening.

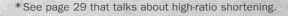

the Basics

CREATING NEW FLAVORS

We do a lot of talk in interviews about the R&D phase, and although we often joke that it mostly consists of "experimenting" in the local bars, it's very difficult to fit our oven through bars' tiny New York door frames, so we are often forced to work elsewhere.

Some cupcakes come easy. The Birthday Cake and Margarita came together almost on the first try, but the Dark 'n Stormy and Old Fashioned went through multiple prototypes. When you're dealing with an iconic flavor profile like an Old Fashioned, it's imperative that you get it just right. An Old Fashioned cupcake can't "kind of taste like" an Old Fashioned. If it doesn't taste just like the cocktail, it's not ready. Most of the time, we eventually get it. Sometimes, though, we have to accept defeat—RIP Tipsy Arnold Palmer.

OHIBITION BAKE

EST. 2011

Unattended miners will be given vodka + Redbull and taught to YOLO.
↓ Boozy CUPCAKES ↓

STOP
U.S.
OFFICIAL

▽

WHAT TO CONSIDER

Our standard menu features 12 flavors, with an additional two or three seasonal cupcakes changed every three months, and five to 10 custom orders a month. At a certain point, there is a real risk of redundancy. How many things can you do with tequila before you're making another Margarita? How many different combinations of whiskey and orange can you put together before you've made just another variation of an Old Fashioned?

When using a product we've already imagined a thousand ways, we take a few things into account:

▶ Who is this product for? If it's for a 20-something's birthday party, we'll likely make something classic and fun that will be relatively easy to recognize. If it's for the brand ambassadors of a specific product, we'll try to find a more creative expression of the product, taking cues from tasting notes, the season, and the brand image. Obviously you want to make something delicious, but a 21-year-old's birthday party might not be the best place for a heavily peated scotch cupcake. Unless, of course, he or she is the coolest 21-year-old on Earth.

▶ What is the season? You want to take the season into account for a couple of reasons. For one, you're going to have a hard time finding good blueberries in the middle of February that don't cost a car payment. For another, a Mojito cupcake just makes more sense in the summer, plus that's when mint is at its best. Ditto to anything with stone fruit or berries. During the fall and winter, apple and pumpkin are big hits, as is anything spiced or mulled.

▶ How will this product be displayed/consumed? Freshness is really the biggest issue here. We have a few items on our menu—as those of you who have visited our store will know—that feature last-minute garnishes. In some cases this is to preserve texture, for example, keeping pretzels crispy and cucumbers juicy. In other cases it is to preserve flavor; for instance, dry (old) citrus zest loses a lot of its oomph. If something is going to be eaten immediately or served as part of an event, those time-sensitive garnishes are delicious and bring an added texture and freshness to the cupcakes. If the cupcakes are going to be consumed at an undetermined or much later time, the garnishes need to be a bit more stable—candies, dried fruits, and chocolate can all work very well. Take it from us— cut fresh fruit is not the way to go if something is going to be sitting out for a few hours. The juice runs out of the fruit into the frosting, resulting in sad fruit and runny frosting. Not a good look.

Sold Out!
see you Tuesday.

FROM CONCEPT TO CUPCAKE

Some of our bestsellers and most famous cupcakes fall into the "conceptual" category, such as our Pretzels & Beer and Scotch & Cigar. The idea itself usually comes at a random time—Brooke literally shot up out of bed when she had the idea for the Scotch & Cigar. Execution tends to be influenced solely by intuition, and individual ingredients often don't make sense until they all come together. Much like a good cocktail, a good cupcake will hit various flavor profiles and textures, all in one bite or sip. Take inspiration from everywhere, and pay attention to patterns. For example, chicken is often served with lemon and rosemary, because lemon and rosemary is a perfect combination. Rosemary also works well with almonds, and almonds pair wonderfully with cranberry. This train of thought led to a lemon, rosemary, almond, and cranberry combination, which turned into such a delicious cupcake that we chose to sell it in the store as a virgin option: L'Italiano. Let your thoughts wander through familiar flavor profiles, and experiment with what comes to mind. The individual cake, filling, and frosting recipes in this book can easily be mixed and matched to re-create almost any cocktail you can think of. Of course, a little editing is necessary, as everything still has to taste good. A Martini cupcake may sound clever, but olive frosting is disgusting no matter how you spin it. Trust us, we've tried.

ARTIFICIAL DYES
(and why we don't use them)

American food would be nothing without food dyes: Commercial bread contains "caramel color," egg yolks are dyed to achieve "optimal" coloring, and, of course, cakes and cupcakes come in every color and, literally, with rainbows. In the early days of Prohibition Bakery, we fell prey to the creative allure of food dyes. We made tie-dye and rainbow-swirled cupcakes for the Broadway opening of *Hair.* We used edible glitter for the opening of *Priscilla, Queen of the Desert.* We did it to customize the cakes for each event, because it's what we thought we were supposed to do.

Then one day, a friend of Leslie's placed an order for a pink and black skull-and-crossbones cake.

This was back when we made cakes. At the time we also used gum paste to make edible sugar decorations in addition to food dyes. We don't do any of those things anymore, thanks to this story.

The cake was to be made out of our Car Bomb recipe—Guinness chocolate cake, whiskey ganache, and Baileys frosting. Our thought was to use hot-pink gum paste for the skull and crossbones, and then use black food dye to make the Baileys frosting black. It would be so edgy.

Black food dye isn't incredibly common, but it does exist. Unlike the food dyes that you can buy at the grocery store, commercial food dyes come in either powder or gel form. Gel dyes are far superior to powdered ones, as they are highly concentrated, so a little goes a very long way. We added a few drops of black dye to the light tan Baileys butter cream, and the whole thing turned a dull gray. So we added more, and a little more, and a little more, but the frosting remained gray. Finally, we just dumped the entire 1-ounce container into the mixing bowl, and our frosting took on a lovely deep-slate color. It was as close to black as we were going to get.

We frosted the cake and put it aside. It was around midnight at this point. As we were cleaning up, each of us got a finger full of leftover frosting and took a quick bite. The amount of dye gave the frosting a slightly metallic taste, very similar to the flavor of a grocery store sheet-cake-frosting rose. We sort of stopped and looked at each other, hoping one of us would think the flavor wasn't such a big deal. It was at that point that we noticed our teeth were black. Upon closer look, we realized our mouths and fingers were dyed as well. The entire kitchen looked like it was covered in soot. We absolutely could not serve the cake, and after unsuccessfully trying to scrape off the offending frosting, we both collapsed in a heap of laughing and/or crying on Brooke's kitchen floor.

We decided at that moment that cakes and colored frosting would not be a part of our future repertoire. That one decision shaped our business more than anything else, because abandoning dyes forced us to find a different way to make our cupcakes stand out. It forced us to look at high-end restaurant plating for decoration ideas, as opposed to other people's cupcakes. Different styles of piping and natural garnishes, ranging from bee pollen to cheddar cheese to black radish, brought an unexpected and elegant twist to each cupcake. As a result, our cupcakes naturally became more upscale and adult, and our product instantly stood out from everyone else's. ▲

FROSTING

While frosting is a particularly polarizing topic for consumers and a weirdly divisive topic for bakers, it is, by definition, simply an emulsification of fat, sugar, and liquid. Frequently, customers are dragged into the store by their boyfriend/girlfriend/tourist pal, walk into the shop, ask a few generic questions, buy a little cupcake, and then stare at it, as if it was a giant risk to take a bite of a teeny cupcake. They look you in the eye as they cautiously peel off the wrapper and state, "I don't generally like frosting," which is code for "I'm just trying to make my loved one happy."

Of course, 95 percent of the time these skeptical customers try one cupcake and end up buying three more because they've finally found a frosting they like. Our frostings are designed to complement the cupcake as a whole, and they have a purpose beyond looking like an Elmo face. This is because we think of the cupcake as a whole flavor experience, not just a cake and a three-inch blob of bright blue frosting.

BUTTER VS. SHORTENING

Throughout this book, you'll notice that some of our frostings use butter and others use shortening. While you can technically interchange the two, shortening is often preferable over butter simply because it is flavorless. When creating a cupcake that has a very distinct flavor, a butter-based frosting will interfere with the flavors in the cupcake. Generally, creamy cocktails—White Russian, Irish Coffee, Grasshopper—lend themselves well to butter-based frostings, whereas fruit-forward cocktails—Margarita, Negroni, Sangria—need a shortening-based frosting.

Shortening, particularly high-ratio shortening,* is also more heat-stable than butter, meaning your cupcakes won't melt in the car on the way to your party. Shortening can also hold more liquid without breaking and remains stable at various textures. So, you can add more or less liquid depending on what sort of frosting decoration you're going for, without worrying that your beautiful rose or swirl is going to wilt in the heat.

You'll also notice that we use toasted meringue frostings for a number of the cupcakes. These cupcakes reflect cocktails that incorporate egg whites for a frothy, creamy effect. Meringue frosting has a similar quality, plus it gives us (and you) an excuse to play with a blowtorch. (And you were worried we weren't going to have any fun.)

The point is that there's more than one way to frost a cake, and different cakes will work better with different frostings. Don't think of frosting as an accessory; think of it as integral to the flavor and balance of each cupcake.

---

*High-ratio shortening differs from traditional shortening, like Crisco, because it contains additional microemulsifiers. That means that high-ratio shortening can hold more sugar and liquid, which is beneficial when you're trying to infuse as much flavor as you can into the frosting. The downside is that many high-ratio brands contain trans fats, but if you do a good-enough web search, you'll find that trans fat-free high-ratio shortening exists.

FROSTING TECHNIQUES

There are a lot of different frostings out there, and we mostly use two at the bakery: American Buttercream and Swiss Meringue. Buttercream is very simple: beat together room-temperature butter or shortening and confectioners' sugar in a stand mixer until chunky, then slowly stream in liquid until the whole thing has a smooth and fluffy consistency. If your frosting is runny, add sugar. If it is too thick, add more liquid. Be sure to cover it (including the tip of the piping bag) when not in use so as to avoid your frosting developing a hard crust.

For the meringue frosting, heat the egg whites, sugar, and cream of tartar over a double boiler* (or for ease of cleaning/transfer, you can heat it in the bowl of your mixer placed over a pot containing an inch of water). Heat egg whites, sugar, and cream of tartar until the sugar is completely dissolved. If you're not certain, rub a little between your fingers. Given that human fingertips can feel imperfections as little as 13 nanometers in size, if there's still undissolved sugar, your fingertips will do a much better job of detecting it than your eyes. If you feel even one grain of sugar, keep whisking the mixture over heat; otherwise you'll end up with a grainy meringue.

Once you're sure all the sugar granules have dissolved, transfer the mixture to your standard mixer and beat on medium speed for two minutes. When the mixture is frothy and beginning to foam, bump up the mixer's speed to high. The meringue is finished when stiff peaks form, meaning that a dollop of the meringue will stand straight up and won't collapse on itself. This could take up to 10 minutes, depending on the strength and speed of your mixer.

Meringues beg to be torched, and Brooke really likes setting things on fire (who doesn't?), so she created a cupcake that involved meringue just so we could regularly use a blowtorch to toast the tops of our meringues. Whether you're using a small crème brûlée torch that you pick up on Amazon.com, or a heavy-duty son of a bitch that's the size of the fire extinguisher you keep close by, you'll have to play around with your torch settings in order to get the hang of toasting without burning. The key is to maintain a low flame and keep the flame's distance many, many inches away from the cupcake. As the heat of the torch gets near the meringue top, the meringue will start to puff. Slowly bring the flame toward the cupcake until it just starts to brown—that's your sweet spot. Any closer and you risk setting a cupcake or ten on fire. Any farther and you won't get that beautiful brown toasted-marshmallow hue.

---

*Double boilers are the slow, annoying "commute" of the pastry world, but they're entirely necessary to get where you want to go. When you place a metal bowl over a simmering pot of water, the heat from the steam warms the bowl and gently transfers heat to the mixture. Not only does this allow for consistent heat throughout, which is important, for example, if you're trying to keep chocolate at a certain temperature, but double boilers also help ensure that ingredients don't burn or curdle. You're welcome to try making meringue frostings in a pot over a regular stove, but we promise you'll end up with a scrambled egg white instead of a silky meringue.

INFUSIONS

One of the best ways to create a new cocktail or put a fun twist on an old one is to introduce infusions. They're cheap, easy, and relatively quick. While you don't want to use any booze that comes in plastic bottles, you don't need to break the bank for infusions. Any mid-grade booze will do. Just keep in mind that although you are adding flavor, you will still taste the base flavor of the alcohol. Shitty rum with mint is still shitty rum.

You can infuse just about any booze, although you'll have your best luck with those that have not already been flavored. Bitters, strongly herbaceous liqueurs, and liqueurs like Baileys and Kahlúa that are artificially flavored, will not absorb additional flavors and should be avoided. Vodka, tequila, rum, whiskey, Scotch, and gin are the way to go. And, if you didn't already know it, gin is basically an infusion—a grain alcohol that has been distilled with any number of additives, depending upon the brand, including juniper, florals, citrus, spices, and even almonds.

We use infusions in a number of cupcakes, from the Mexican Hot Chocolate to the Mojito. Infusions are a great way to evenly distribute a flavor throughout a filling or frosting. The last thing anyone needs is to eat a chile de árbol seed, but a nice infusion allows for the heat without the pain. A mint-infused gin in the frosting of a Pimm's Cup cupcake gives a subtle mint flavor without overpowering the rest of the cupcake. Plus, infusions last forever, so this is a step you'll need to perform only once in a while, depending upon the size of your batches.

HOW TO MAKE YOUR OWN INFUSIONS

1. Choose an infusing agent (rosemary, citrus rinds, ginger, edible flowers, fruit, etc.) to add to your booze of choice.

2. If the infusing agent is small enough, you can add it directly to the bottle of booze. If the infusing ingredients are too big, place them in a clean, appropriately sized, airtight container and then add the booze. For very small ingredients, such as whole spices, fresh herbs, or berries, you can use a mulling bag or a piece of cheesecloth to make retrieval easier, but it is not necessary.

3. Leave the mixture in a cool, dark place. Most infusions will take between 2 and 7 days to make, depending upon the infusing agent, but some can take as little as 20 minutes. Take care with fruits and herbs so that they don't start to brown, which can lend a bitter flavor to the booze. This isn't really a problem for frostings, but it is a problem for sipping.

4. Taste. If the mixture isn't strong enough, switch out the old infusing agents for new ones and let it sit for as long as needed. Repeat as necessary.

INFUSIONS

MINTY RUM OR GIN

This infusion is great for making mojitos without having to worry about getting little bits of mint stuck in your teeth. It also makes a nice addition to a Pimm's Cup.

makes about 3¼ cups

1 (750 milliliter) bottle white rum (or gin)
2 bunches mint

Let the mixture sit for 3 hours, or until mint starts to brown. If it's not minty enough, add fresh mint and let it sit for another 3 hours. Once the flavor is as desired, strain the minted rum (or gin) and discard the mint.

SPICY SCOTCH

Great on the rocks or neat, this is also delicious with
a splash of Coke or soda water.

makes about 3¼ cups

1 (750 milliliter) bottle mid-grade Scotch
3 chiles de árbol

....

Wearing gloves, break the chiles into the Scotch. Let the infusion sit for
20 minutes. Carefully strain the Scotch, discarding all the peppers and
seeds. If it is not spicy enough, add new peppers and let it sit for another
10 minutes, then strain it again. Dispose of chiles. Be sure to wear gloves
and thoroughly scrub your hands after making this one. The last thing you
want is to rub your eye after handling a chile de árbol.

CHERRY VODKA

Obviously this is screaming to be made into a boozy cherry Coke
or Shirley Temple. It's also great with a bit of amaretto and
a splash of cream or club soda.

makes about 3¼ cups

1 (750 milliliter) bottle unflavored vodka
1 cup dried cherries

....

Let the mixture sit for a week. Strain, and discard cherries (or save them for
a grown-up afternoon snack).

FILLINGS

We use a mixture of science and magic to create the boozy fillings for our cupcakes. Now obviously we can't tell you all of our secrets, so although some of these fillings replicate those used in the bakery, a lot of them are reinterpretations that can be created at home relatively easily and inexpensively. Plus, all of these sauces can be easily repurposed with other desserts or cocktails, or as gifts. Don't pretend all of your friends won't be getting Champagne Jelly for Christmas this year.

GANACHE

"Ganache" (pronounced guh-nawsh) is a catchall term for a mixture of finely chopped chocolate melted into warm cream, which, when done correctly, results in a silky smooth, Willy Wonka–worthy bowl of chocolate goodness. While the technique remains the same, ganache ingredient ratios vary widely, depending on the consistency of the desired results. For example, a ganache for a chocolate sauce will require more cream than a ganache intended for chocolate truffle filling. These rules, though, are only applicable to milk and dark chocolate ganache. White chocolate ganache is another issue entirely.

For your reference:

- **Filling/glaze** (what we use for our ganache filling): 1:1 ratio of chocolate to cream, by weight.

- **Frosting**: 1:2 ratio of chocolate to cream

- **Truffles**: 2:1 ratio of chocolate to cream (We don't make truffles, but consider this advice a thank-you for your purchase of the book)

But first things first. When making a ganache, make sure your bowl and tools are completely dry. Just a drop or two of water will ruin the whole thing. Once your chocolate and cream are combined, then you can whisk in butter, flavoring, or booze as needed to reach the consistency or flavor you desire.

But, of course, it's not that simple. Ganache can be a delicious pain in the ass because it's highly temperature sensitive. Ganache likes to sit between 90°F and 110°F (this is where that digital thermometer comes in handy). Heat the cream too much and not only do you scald the cream, but the hot cream can cause the cocoa butter in the chocolate to get too hot, which creates pooled puddles of fat that separate from the rest of the mixture and result in a grainy, "broken" texture. The best way to avoid this atrocity is to let the cream and chocolate hang out and get to know each other for at least a minute before you get involved with a spatula or whisk. After a minute, begin whisking, but stop as soon as the mixture comes together. Excessive stirring can cause the mixture to fall below 90°F too quickly, which can also result in a grainy texture.

Sometimes, you think you do everything right and the damn ganache still breaks. The good news is that one of the easiest ways to fix a broken ganache is to add alcohol, and since we are boozy bakers, we add alcohol to everything. Rejoice! When making your ganache, if you begin to notice that it's not looking so smooth (little bits of separated chocolate will start to stick to the sides of the bowl), just grab the appropriate booze and start to stream it in. The key word here is "stream." Start slow, and stay slow. Dumping it in all at once is not going to help you. We could explain the science behind this, but let's just use this analogy instead: when you get into a hot tub, you get in slowly and let your body acclimate to the heat so you don't shock your entire system. The same thing goes for adding booze to a ganache—just go a little at a time so it all gently melds together.

The moral of our ganache story is: take your time and pay attention, but understand that you probably will break a ganache or two in your lifetime. Luckily, they can be fixed, either with booze or various other methods that can be found on the Internet by searching for "broken ganache."

BITTERSWEET OR MILK CHOCOLATE GANACHE

Although we suggest adding booze to most fillings when they have cooled, with ganache you're going to want to add it while it's still warm, right after you've completely mixed in the butter. The ganache will have cooled enough not to cook out the alcohol and will still be soft enough to fully incorporate the liquid easily. This recipe is meant to be repurposed with whichever booze is applicable for each cupcake.

makes 1¼ cups

⅓ cup heavy cream
4 ounces (113 g) finely chopped bittersweet or milk chocolate
1 tablespoon unsalted butter
½ cup booze

1. Simmer cream over medium heat until it is just bubbling. Take care not to boil it.

2. Meanwhile, chop bittersweet chocolate into chunks and transfer it to a bowl.

3. When cream is heated, pour it over room-temperature chocolate.

4. Let the chocolate and cream mixture sit for a minute or so, and then whisk. When it is smooth, add the butter. Ganache should be glossy.

5. While whisking, stream in your booze of choice until it is incorporated. The mixture will be very thin.

6. Transfer the ganache to a squeeze bottle and refrigerate.

7. Cool completely before filling cupcakes.

You'll find adaptations of this basic boozy ganache in the recipes for the Port in the Storm (page 225), Monkey Business (page 108), and Campfire (page 246) cupcakes. In order to create fillings for each of the aforementioned cupcakes, follow steps 1–4, stirring in ruby port, banana liqueur, or Guinness, respectively. To make the Mexican Hot Chocolate filling, you'll want to begin by simmering the cream in step 1 with two dried chiles de árbol. You will then follow the rest of the steps, taking the added step of straining the cream over the chocolate rather than simply pouring it over. Then stir in Spicy Scotch (page 35) until smooth.

WHITE CHOCOLATE GANACHE

Ganache made with white chocolate is significantly finickier than a ganache made with milk or dark chocolate. Unlike milk or dark chocolate ganaches, you can't fiddle with the ratio of chocolate to cream as easily; otherwise the ganache simply won't work in the same way.

makes 1¾ cups

6 ounces white chocolate
¼ cup heavy cream
1 cup booze

1. In a saucepan, combine white chocolate and heavy cream.
2. Over low heat, constantly stir the mixture until all the white chocolate is melted.
3. Remove from heat and slowly drizzle in booze while whisking.
4. Transfer the ganache to a squeeze bottle and refrigerate. Do not use until completely cool.

SAGE GANACHE

Sage and chocolate are a wonderful, highly underutilized combination. In this recipe, we follow the standard method for ganache, using a sage-infused cream. Because the cream is reduced so as to intensify the sage flavor, we thin the ganache with a beer reduction, so the ganache stays silky.

makes 1½ cups

1 bottle of beer
6 large sage leaves
1 cup heavy cream
2 ounces bittersweet chocolate
2 ounces milk chocolate
1 tablespoon unsalted butter

....

1. In a saucepan, bring beer to a boil, and let it boil until it has reduced by half, keeping a close watch.* Remove from heat and let cool.

2. Add sage leaves to cream, and simmer over medium heat until reduced by half. Take care not to boil.

3. Meanwhile, chop bittersweet and milk chocolate into fine chunks. When the cream is heated, strain and pour it over the room-temperature chocolate.

4. Let the chocolate and cream mixture sit for a minute or two, and then whisk. When smooth, add the butter.

5. Slowly whisk in beer reduction.

6. Transfer the ganache to a squeeze bottle and set it aside.

* Seriously, watch the beer. In just seconds, this stuff will foam up like a science project and leave you with a huge mess.

BOOZY JAMS AND JELLIES

Making a boozy jelly is the best way to convey a strong, singular flavor, such as in liqueur or wine fillings, which is why you'll find them being used for a lot of the more literal cupcakes in the book (such as the Pisco Sour and Sex on the Beach). It also works beautifully for the more fruit-forward drinks as a way to incorporate the booze in a delicious and balanced manner. The most important thing when making a jelly is to bring everything to a full boil before and after adding the pectin, while not overcooking the mixture. More than a couple of minutes of heating after the second boil can result in jelly that is sticky and not as good for filling (or spreading on toast, for that matter).

WHISKEY FIG JAM

▼

This makes the most delicious cupcake filling, but be sure to save some to make manchego jamón sandwiches later. If you use dried figs for this, be sure to add the additional whiskey.

makes 2 cups

1 pound fresh figs, or ½ pound dried figs and 1 cup whiskey
1 tablespoon lemon zest
½ cup whiskey
½ cup sugar

....

1. If using dried figs, place figs in a shallow container and cover them completely with 1 cup whiskey. The next day, strain the mixture and keep the discarded liquid. Congratulations: you just made fig-infused whiskey!

2. Add fresh or soaked figs to a food processor along with zest and ½ cup whiskey.

3. Process until figs are finely chopped.

4. Add the mixture to a saucepan along with sugar, and cook over high heat, stirring constantly.

5. Bring the mixture to boil, and continue to stir until sugar is completely dissolved, 3–5 minutes.

6. Once sugar is dissolved, reduce heat to medium-high and continue cooking for another 3–5 minutes.

7. Remove from heat and transfer to a heat-proof, airtight container.

SPARKLING WINE OR WHITE WINE JELLY

▼

Whether you're making this jelly with white wine or bubbly, we don't recommend wasting the good stuff, because you're just going to drown it in sugar. Really, any drinkable white or sparkling wine will do. Drink the good stuff after you've managed to make all of these delicious cupcakes without setting anything on fire.

makes 3 cups

2 cups wine
3 cups sugar
$1/2$ teaspoon lemon zest
1 (3 ounce) package liquid pectin

1. Combine wine and sugar in a saucepan.

2. Heat on medium-high heat until the mixture comes to a boil.

3. Add zest and pectin and bring to a boil, stirring constantly.

4. Remove jelly from heat and skim off any foam.

5. Transfer jelly to a heat-proof, airtight container.

LIQUEUR JELLY

▼

For use with liqueurs such as amaretto, pisco, Pimm's, crème de violette, etc.

makes 1½ cups

1½ cups liqueur
2 cups sugar
1 (3 ounce) package liquid pectin

The Day Before

1. Combine liqueur and sugar in a saucepan.
2. Heat on medium-high until the mixture comes to a boil.
3. Add pectin and stir until dissolved.
4. Bring the mixture to a hard boil and boil for 1 minute, stirring constantly.
5. Remove the mixture from heat and skim off any foam. Transfer to a clean, heat-proof container and let it set in the refrigerator overnight.

The Day Of

1. Bring jelly to the correct consistency by whisking in additional liqueur by the tablespoon.
2. Transfer jelly to a squeeze bottle.

GINGER BEER JELLY

▼

Soda jellies can be found in some cookbooks from the 1930s, but they've long since been forgotten. Any ginger beer will work for this jelly. Use a bourgie ginger beer with bits of ginger floating on the bottom if you want to get all fancy with it.

makes 3 cups

1½ cups ginger beer
3 cups sugar
1 (3 ounce) package liquid pectin

....

1. Add ginger beer and sugar to a saucepan.

2. Heat over medium-high heat until the mixture boils, stirring constantly.

3. Add pectin and stir until dissolved.

4. Bring the mixture back up to a boil, and stir for another minute.

5. Remove from heat and skim off any foam.

6. Transfer the mixture to a heat-proof, airtight container.

CITRUS JELLY

▼

Marmalade isn't just for your grandpa's toast anymore. You'll notice this recipe includes significantly less pectin than some of our other jellies. Citrus rind and apple are both great sources of natural pectin, so because this recipe includes plenty of zest for flavor, you'll need less pectin to get the right consistency. You can use the recipe below to make any citrus jelly, but for clarity's sake, we'll use the example of an orange jelly.

makes 1¼ cups

1 lemon
2 oranges *(or whatever citrus fruit
the cupcake recipe calls for)*
1 cup water
2 cups sugar
½ (1.5 ounce) package liquid pectin

···

1. Zest lemon and oranges. Set aside.

2. Juice both oranges, which should net you about 1 cup of orange juice.

3. Add orange juice, water, and sugar to a saucepan.

4. Heat on medium-high heat, stirring constantly.

5. Bring to a boil, then add lemon and orange zest and pectin.

6. Boil the mixture for at least one minute, stirring constantly.

7. Skim off any foam that may be on top.

8. Transfer the mixture to a heat-proof, airtight container to cool.

HARD CIDER JELLY

▼

While most of our cupcake recipes call for a jam or jelly made with pectin, some call for a filling that is as pure as you can get it. In order to avoid adding extra sugar to this hard cider filling, we use gelatin instead of pectin.

makes 2 cups

4 teaspoons unflavored powdered gelatin
2 cups tart hard cider, plus more as needed
1½ tablespoons lemon juice

·····································

The Day Before

1. Soften gelatin by sprinkling it over ½ cup of cider. Let the mixture sit for 20 minutes.
2. Bring remaining 1½ cups cider to a boil; remove from heat.
3. Add the softened gelatin mixture to the hot cider, stirring to dissolve.
4. Add lemon juice.
5. Bring to a full rolling boil.
6. Transfer the mixture to a container and refrigerate overnight.

The Day Of

1. Transfer gelled cider to a food processor and pulse until smooth.
2. If the mixture is too thick, stream in additional hard cider until a pourable consistency is reached.
3. Transfer to a squeeze bottle. Do not refrigerate. It will last for 3 days.

WHEAT BEER JELLY

▼

You can use this for any beer jelly/cupcake combination, though you'll want to swap out the orange juice for more beer if you're using something other than a wheat beer. Orange is featured in this recipe as it pairs well with wheat beers—think of the iconic orange slice floating in a Hoegaarden.

makes 1½ cups

4 teaspoons unflavored powdered gelatin
2 cups wheat beer
1 ½ tablespoons orange juice

The Day Before

1. Soften gelatin by sprinkling it over ½ cup of beer. Let the mixture sit for 20 minutes.

2. Bring remaining 1½ cups beer to a boil. Remove from heat.

3. Add the softened gelatin mixture to the hot beer, stirring to dissolve.

4. Add orange juice to the mixture.

5. Bring to a full rolling boil.

6. Transfer the mixture to a container and refrigerate overnight.

The Day Of

1. Transfer gelled beer to a food processor, and pulse until smooth.

2. If the mixture is too thick, stream in additional beer until a pourable consistency is reached.

3. Transfer to a squeeze bottle. Do not refrigerate. It will last for 3 days.

INFUSED JELLY

▼

Infused jellies are a great way to bring a more subtle flavor, such as mint or tea, to the forefront. Just be sure to make them extra strong so they don't get lost when the sugar is added (brew triple-strong tea, or use one bunch of mint per cup of water).

makes 3 cups

2 cups heavily infused liquid
2 cups sugar
1 (3 ounce) package liquid pectin

....

Up to a Few Days Before

1. Place the aromatic in a saucepan and gently mash it down as much as possible to release flavor.

2. Add water and bring to a boil.

3. Remove from heat, cover, and let steep for 45 minutes.

4. Strain into an airtight container before refrigerating.

The Day Before

1. Add aromatic infusion and sugar to a clean saucepan. Bring to a boil.

2. Add pectin and stir until dissolved.

3. Bring the mixture to a hard boil and boil for 1 minute, stirring constantly.

4. Remove the mixture from heat and skim off any foam. Transfer to a clean, heat-proof container and let it set in the refrigerator overnight.

The Day Of

1. Whisk aromatic jelly until smooth. The consistency should be like thick syrup.

2. Add additional aromatic infusions or booze by the tablespoon until the desired consistency is reached.

3. Transfer the jelly to a squeeze bottle.

COFFEE JELLY
▼

This is very similar to Infused Jelly, in that it allows for a more pronounced coffee flavor than one could hope for from adding coffee to a cake or frosting. It's perfect for the White Russian cupcake, but could also be used for an Irish Coffee or Black Russian cocktail.

makes 3 cups

2 cups brewed coffee
2 cups sugar
1 (3 ounce) package liquid pectin

1. Bring coffee and sugar to a boil in a saucepan.
2. Add in pectin.
3. Bring to a boil for at least another minute, stirring constantly.
4. Skim off any foam and transfer the mixture to an airtight container.
5. Store in refrigerator overnight.

RED WINE JELLY
▼

The biggest consideration when making red wine jelly is which sort of red wine to use. For the Red Sangria cupcake on page 220, for example, you'll want to use a mild, fruity red wine that won't clash with the subtle citrus flavors in the cake. Merlot is probably your best bet.

makes 4 cups

2 cups wine
2 cups sugar
2 tablespoons orange juice
2 tablespoons lemon juice
1 (3 ounce) package liquid pectin

1. Add wine, sugar, and juices to a saucepan.
2. Cook on medium-high heat until the mixture starts to boil.
3. Add pectin and cook for another minute, stirring constantly.
4. Remove from heat and skim off any foam.
5. Transfer the mixture to a heatproof, airtight container and refrigerate overnight.

CHERRY JELLY

▼

Some cupcakes benefit from a purer cherry flavor, which is best conveyed with a puree (p. 51), but a subtler cherry flavor can be achieved with the use of a jelly.

makes 3 cups

2 cups tart cherry juice
2 cups sugar
1 (3 ounce) package liquid pectin

1. Combine juice and sugar in a saucepan. Bring to a boil, stirring frequently.
2. Add pectin and stir until dissolved.
3. Bring the mixture to a hard boil and boil for 1 minute, stirring constantly.
4. Remove from heat and skim off any foam.
5. Transfer to a clean, heat-proof container and let set in the refrigerator overnight.

SAUCES

If you haven't figured it out by now, our mantra is "when in doubt, add more booze." This section is a catchall for a few more fillings to booze up, including purees, fruit sauces, and caramels. All of these can easily be repurposed for other desserts, and the purees can be used in cocktails as a less sugary alternative to juice or syrup.

FRUIT PUREE

Fruit purees are a lesson in not messing with something that is damn near perfect. Few things are as life affirming as picking a fresh blackberry and eating it right on the spot. When you're making a particularly fresh and not-too-sweet cocktail or cupcake, using a berry puree instead of a berry jelly can elevate the entire thing. You can use any berry or any combination of berries when making your puree. Just be sure to honor seasonality because there is no comparison between a seasonal summer berry and one that is genetically engineered to grow under a UV lamp during the winter months. Before making your puree, consider its ultimate cupcake destiny, and alter the booze and berries accordingly. If you're unsure of what you're going to make, or if you are making a virgin cupcake, you can substitute water for the booze.

makes 1 cup puree, ¾ cup juice

12 ounces fresh berries *(blackberries, blueberries, etc.)*
1¼ cups booze of choice

....

1. Combine fruit and booze in a saucepan.

2. Over medium heat, slowly bring the mixture to a soft boil and let it simmer until the fruit breaks down, about 5 minutes.

3. Remove from heat and strain out berries, reserving the fruit-infused liquid for future use.

4. Transfer fruit to a food processor, and blend until smooth.

5. Store puree in the refrigerator in an airtight container until ready to use.

PINEAPPLE SAUCE

▼

This is quite possibly the easiest sauce recipe you'll ever find, but it can also be very easy to mess up, so you'll want to use a candy thermometer to monitor the temperature and make sure you don't go from pineapple sauce to pineapple candies.

makes ¾ cup

1 cup diced pineapple
1 cup sugar

....

1. Puree 1 cup pineapple.
2. Heat pureed pineapple and sugar in a saucepan over low/medium heat.
3. Cook for about 5 minutes, or until it reaches 220°F. The mixture will be very thick.
4. Remove the mixture from heat and transfer it to an airtight, heat-proof container.
5. Allow the mixture to cool slightly; then stir in booze of choice.

CARAMEL SAUCE

▼

Caramel sauce is probably the most traditional sauce to booze up. Who hasn't had bread pudding, pecan pie, or brownies with a bourbon-caramel sauce? But that doesn't mean that all boozy caramels are created equal. Much like mixing drinks, the simplicity of caramel leaves a lot of room for exploration. To make a nice dark rummy caramel sauce, add a little dark brown sugar to mirror the molasses of the rum. If you're making a whiskey caramel, try using 1 part honey to 4 parts white sugar to bring out the honeyed undertones. And if you're looking to making a basic caramel sauce, stick with white sugar. Any leftover sauce can be added to coffee, poured over ice cream, or used as filling for delicious sandwich cookies.

makes 1½ cups

1 cup sugar
4 tablespoons (2 ounces) butter
½ cup heavy cream
1 pinch salt
¼ cup booze of choice

1. In a saucepan, heat sugar and butter over medium heat until butter is melted and the mixture appears smooth (not grainy). After a few minutes, the mixture will bubble and turn a nice golden color.

2. While the sugar and butter mixture is melting, warm cream over low heat, taking care not to boil it.

3. When sugar is fully dissolved in the sugar/butter mixture, slowly stream in warm cream, stirring constantly.

4. Add pinch of salt and stir thoroughly.

5. Once everything is fully mixed, slowly pour in booze, stirring constantly until the mixture is smooth and even in color.

6. The caramel will appear thin when hot, but will thicken significantly when cooled.

7. Transfer the boozy caramel to a squeeze bottle, and let it cool before filling.

APPLESAUCE

▼

You can use bottled applesauce, but you'll want to cook it down over medium heat for about 10 minutes to thicken it. We suggest you make your own, following the recipe below, using your favorite apples and adjusting sweetness to your taste. A mix of apple varities will give you the best flavor.

makes 3 cups

a shit-ton of apples, cored, peeled, and pureed*
zest of 1 lemon
1 cup water
3/4 cup granulated sugar
1 tablespoon cinnamon
1/4 teaspoon salt

....

1. Peel, core, and quarter apples.

2. Transfer apples to large pot with lemon zest, water, sugar, cinnamon, and salt.

3. Bring to a boil over high heat.

4. Reduce to a simmer and cover. Simmer for 20–30 minutes, or until apples can be easily stabbed through with a fork.

5. Remove from heat and allow to cool.

6. Pour apples into a blender and puree until there are no more large chunks. If your blender is on the smaller side, puree in batches.

7. Transfer applesauce to an airtight container. It will keep in the refrigerator for up to 3 weeks.

---

*Okay, really 4–5 medium-sized apples, but it'll feel like a shit-ton by the time you're done coring and peeling.

CITRUS CURD

▼

Curd is a great way to incorporate a tart citrus flavor
into your cupcake without overwhelming the other flavors.
Lemon, lime, and passion fruit are particularly effective.

makes 3 cups

4 tablespoons butter
1½ cups sugar
4 eggs
enough fruit *(lemon, lime, orange, etc.)* to yield ¼ cup juice
⅛ teaspoon salt
½ teaspoon citrus zest

1. Cream butter and sugar in the bowl of a standing mixer.
2. Add eggs one at a time, beating thoroughly between the addition of
   each egg.
3. Zest one fruit to yield ½ teaspoon of zest, and set aside.
4. Juice fruit to yield ¼ cup juice.
5. Add citrus juice 1 tablespoon at a time.
6. Add salt. The mixture may appear curdled (lumpy), but it will smooth
   out once heated.
7. Transfer the mixture to a saucepan and cook over low heat for about
   10 minutes, stirring constantly.
8. Stir in zest.
9. Remove the mixture from heat and transfer it to a heat-proof container.
10. Let it cool on the counter before refrigerating.

Vodka

The dude abides.

WHITE RUSSIAN

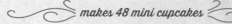

makes 48 mini cupcakes

CAKE

1	egg
⅓ cup (75 g)	sour cream
1⅓ cup (166 g)	all-purpose flour
1 cup (200 g)	granulated sugar
¾ teaspoon	baking soda
1 tablespoon	espresso powder
½ teaspoon	salt
½ cup (115 g)	brewed coffee
1 stick (115 g)	butter, unsalted

FILLING

1 cup (230 g)	Coffee Jelly (page 49)
⅓ cup (80 g)	vodka

FROSTING

1 stick (115 g)	butter, unsalted
1 pound	confectioners' sugar
⅓ cup (80 g)	Kahlua

GARNISH

coffee bean

TO MAKE THE CAKE

1. Preheat the oven to 325°F. Line mini cupcake tins with paper liners.

2. In the bowl of an electric mixer, beat egg and sour cream.

3. In another bowl, combine flour, sugar, baking soda, espresso powder, and salt. Set aside.

4. Combine coffee and butter in a saucepan and heat until the butter melts.

5. Remove from heat. With the mixer running on low, slowly pour the hot coffee/butter mixture into the mixing bowl with the egg/sour cream mixture. Beat until incorporated.

6. Slowly add the dry ingredients to the wet ingredients and beat until incorporated.

7. Fill cupcake tins two-thirds full.

8. Bake for 10 minutes. Let cupcakes cool completely on a wire rack before filling or frosting.

TO MAKE THE FILLING

1. Whisk Coffee Jelly in a bowl until smooth.

2. Add vodka 1 tablespoon at a time, stirring thoroughly between additions.

3. Transfer the Coffee Jelly/vodka mixture to a squeeze bottle.

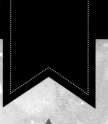

TO MAKE THE FROSTING

1. With an electric mixer, beat butter with the paddle attachment until fluffy.

2. With the mixture on low speed, slowly add confectioners' sugar until combined.

3. Slowly stream in Kahlua and beat until smooth and fluffy, with no lumps or air bubbles.

4. Transfer the frosting to a piping bag.

ASSEMBLY

1. When cupcakes are cool, core each cupcake with a small pastry tip. If you don't have a pastry tip, poke a hole in the middle of the cupcake with a narrow-bladed knife (a steak knife will do).

2. Fill the cavity with Coffee Jelly/vodka filling, taking care not to let it overflow.

3. Frost cupcakes to your liking.

4. Garnish with a single coffee bean.

This cupcake is based on the Birthday Cake shot, which is equal parts lemon vodka and Frangelico served in a sugar-rimmed glass. Though we don't tend to encourage mixed shots (only straight whiskey and tequila for us, please and thank you), this one is so meta that we just we had to make it.

BIRTHDAY CAKE

Gone to buy a caple handles of vodka, be back in 10 mins.
—Thanks mgmt.

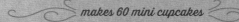

makes 60 mini cupcakes

CAKE

1⅔ cup (208 g)	all-purpose flour
1½ teaspoons	baking powder
½ teaspoon	baking soda
¼ teaspoon	salt
1 cup (240 g)	plain yogurt
⅓ cup (70 g)	olive oil
1 cup (200 g)	granulated sugar
¼ cup (60 g)	lemon juice
2 teaspoons	lemon zest
2	eggs

FILLING

1 cup (230 g)	lemon curd (see Citrus Curd, page 55)
3 tablespoons (40 g)	vodka

FROSTING

1 stick (115 g)	butter, unsalted
1 pound	confectioners' sugar
⅓ cup (80 g)	Frangelico

GARNISH

zest of 1 lemon
1 cup sugar

TO MAKE THE CAKE

1. Preheat the oven to 325°F. Line mini cupcake tins with paper liners.

2. Place flour, baking powder, baking soda, and salt in a bowl and combine. Set aside.

3. Combine yogurt, olive oil, sugar, lemon juice, and lemon zest in the mixing bowl of a stand mixer and beat until incorporated.

4. With the mixer running, add eggs one at a time.

5. With the mixer on slow speed, slowly add the dry mixture to the wet ingredients in the mixing bowl.

6. Mix until just combined, taking care not to overbeat.

7. Fill cupcake tins to the halfway point.

8. Bake for 10 minutes. Let cupcakes cool completely on a wire rack before filling or frosting.

TO MAKE THE FILLING

1. Whisk lemon curd in a bowl until smooth.

2. Add vodka 1 tablespoon at a time, stirring thoroughly between additions.

3. Transfer the lemon curd/vodka mixture to a squeeze bottle.

TO MAKE THE FROSTING

1. With an electric mixer, beat butter with the paddle attachment until it is fluffy.

2. With the mixer on low speed, slowly add confectioners' sugar until combined.

3. Slowly stream in Frangelico and beat until smooth and fluffy, with no lumps or air bubbles.

4. Transfer the frosting to a piping bag.

TO MAKE THE GARNISH

1. Pulse the zest/sugar mixture in a food processor until fine.

2. Store in an airtight container; it will keep indefinitely. If the flavor diminishes, add fresh lemon zest.

ASSEMBLY

1. When cupcakes are cool, core each cupcake with a small pastry tip. If you don't have a pastry tip, poke a hole in the middle of the cupcake with a narrow-bladed knife (a steak knife will do).

2. Fill the cavity with the lemon curd/vodka mixture, taking care not to let it overflow.

3. Frost to your liking.

4. Sprinkle with lemon sugar.

makes 60 mini cupcakes

CAKE

1²/₃ cups (208 g)	all-purpose flour
1¹/₂ teaspoons	baking powder
¹/₂ teaspoon	baking soda
¹/₄ teaspoon	salt
1 cup (240 g)	plain yogurt
¹/₃ cup (70 g)	olive oil
1 cup (200 g)	granulated sugar
¹/₄ cup (60 g)	lemon juice
2 teaspoons	lemon zest
2	eggs

FILLING

1 cup (230 g)	blueberry* puree with vodka (see Fruit Puree, page 51)
¹/₄ cup (60 g)	vodka

FROSTING

¹/₂ cup (115 g)	shortening
1 pound	confectioners' sugar
2¹/₂ tablespoons (40 g)	blueberry juice, reserved from berry puree
2¹/₂ tablespoons (40 g)	vodka
1 teaspoon	lemon zest

GARNISH

fresh blueberries

---

* Use only fresh blueberries, as frozen ones will hold
too much water—by that we mean you're only allowed
to make this in the summertime, when blueberries
are actually in season.

BOOZY BLUEBERRY LEMONADE

Sometimes, there's no need to mess with a classic,
beyond adding booze to it. Lemonade is delicious.
Blueberries are delicious. Vodka is fun. Therefore,
lemonade + blueberries + vodka = delicious fun.

TO MAKE THE CAKE

1. Preheat the oven to 325°F. Line mini cupcake tins with paper liners.
2. Place flour, baking powder, baking soda, and salt in a bowl and combine. Set aside.
3. Combine yogurt, olive oil, sugar, lemon juice, and lemon zest in the mixing bowl of a stand mixer, and beat until incorporated.
4. With the mixer running, add eggs one at a time.
5. With the mixer on low speed, slowly add the dry ingredients to the wet ingredients in the mixing bowl.
6. Mix until just combined, taking care not to overbeat.
7. Fill cupcake tins to the halfway point.
8. Bake for 10 minutes. Let cupcakes cool completely on a wire rack before filling or frosting.

TO MAKE THE FILLING

1. Whisk blueberry puree in a bowl until smooth.
2. Add vodka 1 tablespoon at a time, stirring thoroughly between additions.
3. Transfer the blueberry puree/vodka mixture to a squeeze bottle.

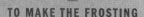

TO MAKE THE FROSTING

1. With an electric mixer, beat shortening with the paddle attachment until it is fluffy.
2. With the mixer on low speed, slowly add confectioners' sugar until combined.
3. Slowly stream in blueberry juice, vodka, and zest, and beat until smooth and fluffy, with no lumps or air bubbles.
4. Transfer the frosting to a piping bag.

ASSEMBLY

1. When cupcakes are cool, core each cupcake with a small pastry tip. If you don't have a pastry tip, poke a hole in the middle of the cupcake with a narrow-bladed knife (a steak knife will do).
2. Use a squeeze bottle to fill the cavity with the blueberry puree/vodka mixture, taking care not to let it overflow.
3. Frost cupcakes to your liking.
4. Garnish with a fresh blueberry.

COSMO

Though no longer on our menu, the Cosmo was technically our inaugural cupcake flavor. Initially created as a cake for Brooke's friend's bachelorette party,* the Cosmo paved the boozy cupcake path. Gone but not forgotten, little buddy.

* Hi Heather!

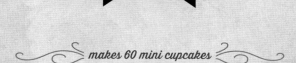

makes 60 mini cupcakes

CAKE

1²⁄₃ cups (208 g)	all-purpose flour
1¹⁄₂ teaspoons	baking powder
¹⁄₂ teaspoon	baking soda
¹⁄₄ teaspoon	salt
1 cup (240 g)	plain yogurt
¹⁄₃ cup (70 g)	olive oil
1 cup (200 g)	granulated sugar
¹⁄₄ cup (60 g)	lime juice
2 teaspoons	lime zest
2	eggs

FILLING

1 cup (230 g)	cranberry puree with vodka (see Fruit Puree, page 51)
¹⁄₄ cup (60 g)	vodka

FROSTING

1 stick (115 g)	butter, unsalted
1 pound	confectioners' sugar
¹⁄₃ cup (80 g)	triple sec, reserved from filling
1 teaspoon	orange zest

TO MAKE THE CAKE

1. Preheat the oven to 325°F. Line mini cupcake tins with paper liners.

2. Place flour, baking powder, baking soda, and salt in a bowl and combine. Set aside.

3. Combine yogurt, olive oil, sugar, lime juice, and lime zest in the mixing bowl of a stand mixer, and beat until incorporated.

4. With the mixer running, add eggs one at a time.

5. With the mixer on low speed, slowly add the dry ingredients to the wet ingredients in the mixing bowl.

6. Mix until just combined, taking care not to overbeat.

7. Fill cupcake tins to the halfway point.

8. Bake for 10 minutes. Let cupcakes cool completely on a wire rack before filling or frosting.

TO MAKE THE FILLING

1. Whisk cranberry puree in a bowl until smooth.
2. Add vodka one tablespoon at a time, stirring thoroughly after each addition.
3. Transfer the cranberry puree/vodka mixture to a squeeze bottle.

TO MAKE THE FROSTING

1. With an electric mixer, beat butter with the paddle attachment until fluffy.
2. With the mixer on low speed, slowly add confectioners' sugar until combined.
3. Slowly stream in triple sec and beat until smooth and fluffy, with no lumps or air bubbles.
4. Add orange zest and beat until fully incorporated.
5. Transfer the frosting to a piping bag.

ASSEMBLY

1. When cupcakes are cool, core each cupcake with a small pastry tip. If you don't have a pastry tip, poke a hole in the middle of the cupcake with a narrow-bladed knife (a steak knife will do).
2. Fill the cavity with the cranberry puree/vodka mixture, taking care not to let it overflow.
3. Frost cupcakes to your liking.

ROYAL BLUSH

The Royal Blush isn't actually a Prohibition-era cocktail, though the name and ingredients would imply otherwise. Created in the early aughts by Eben Freeman of Tailor Restaurant in New York City, this cocktail is perfectly suited for summer, which is also when you'll find the best-quality fresh cherries and mint.

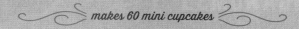
makes 60 mini cupcakes

CAKE

1²/₃ cups (208 g)	all-purpose flour
1¹/₂ teaspoons	baking powder
¹/₂ teaspoon	baking soda
¹/₄ teaspoon	salt
1 cup (240 g)	plain yogurt
¹/₃ cup (70 g)	olive oil
1 cup (200 g)	granulated sugar
¹/₄ cup (60 g)	lime juice
zest	¹/₄ lime
2	eggs

FILLING

1 cup (230 g)	mint-infused jelly (see Infused Jelly, page 48)
¹/₄ cup (60 g)	Cherry Vodka (page 35)

FROSTING

¹/₂ cup (115 g)	shortening
1 pound	confectioners' sugar
2¹/₂ tablespoons (40 g)	sparkling wine
2¹/₂ tablespoons (40 g)	cherry juice

GARNISH

fresh mint

TO MAKE THE CAKE

1. Preheat the oven to 325°F. Line mini cupcake tins with paper liners.
2. Place flour, baking powder, baking soda, and salt in a bowl and combine. Set aside.
3. Combine yogurt, olive oil, sugar, lime juice, and lime zest in the mixing bowl of a stand mixer and beat until incorporated.
4. With the mixer running, add eggs one at a time.
5. With the mixer on low speed, slowly add the dry ingredients to the wet ingredients in the mixing bowl.
6. Mix until just combined, taking care not to overbeat.
7. Fill cupcake tins to the halfway point.
8. Bake for 10 minutes. Let cupcakes cool completely on a wire rack before filling or frosting.

TO MAKE THE FILLING

1. Whisk the mint-infused jelly until smooth.
2. Add in Cherry Vodka 1 tablespoon at a time, stirring thoroughly between additions.
3. Transfer the mint-infused jelly/Cherry Vodka mixture to a squeeze bottle.

TO MAKE THE FROSTING

1. With an electric mixer, beat shortening with the paddle attachment until fluffy.

2. With the mixer on low speed, slowly add confectioners' sugar until combined.

3. Slowly stream in sparkling wine and cherry juice, and beat until smooth and fluffy, with no lumps or air bubbles.

4. Transfer the frosting to a piping bag.

ASSEMBLY

1. When cupcakes are cool, core each cupcake with a small pastry tip. If you don't have a pastry tip, poke a hole in the middle of the cupcake with a narrow-bladed knife (a steak knife will do).

2. Fill each cavity with the mint-infused jelly/Cherry Vodka mixture, taking care not to let it overflow.

3. Frost to your liking.

4. Garnish with a fresh mint leaf.

SEX ON THE BEACH

Although we suggest garnishing these cupcakes with fresh peaches, keep our rules for garnishing in mind (see page 24). In other words, if the cupcakes are going to be sitting out for a while, you'll want to use dried peaches or skip the garnish altogether.

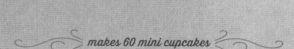

makes 60 mini cupcakes

CAKE

1 2/3 cups (208 g)	all-purpose flour
1 1/2 teaspoons	baking powder
1/2 teaspoon	baking soda
1/4 teaspoon	salt
1 cup (240 g)	plain yogurt
1/3 cup (70 g)	olive oil
1 cup (200 g)	granulated sugar
1/4 cup (60 g)	orange juice
2 teaspoons	orange zest
2	eggs

FILLING

1 cup (230 g)	peach schnapps jelly (see Liqueur Jelly, page 43)
1/4 cup (60 g)	vodka

FROSTING

1/2 cup (115 g)	shortening
1 pound	confectioners' sugar
1/3 cup (80 g)	cranberry juice*

GARNISH

small peach cubes
lemon or orange juice

---

*Not "cranberry juice drink" or any other "cranberry juice cocktail" that has more than one ingredient (100% cranberries) listed.

TO MAKE THE CAKE

1. Preheat the oven to 325°F. Line mini cupcake tins with paper liners.
2. Place flour, baking powder, baking soda, and salt in a bowl and combine. Set aside.
3. Combine yogurt, olive oil, sugar, orange juice, and orange zest in the mixing bowl of a stand mixer and beat until incorporated.
4. With the mixer running, add eggs one at a time.
5. With the mixer on low speed, slowly add the dry ingredients to the wet ingredients in the mixing bowl.
6. Mix until just combined, taking care not to overbeat.
7. Fill cupcake tins to the halfway point.
8. Bake for 10 minutes. Let cupcakes cool completely on a wire rack before filling or frosting.

TO MAKE THE FILLING

1. Whisk peach schnapps jelly until smooth.
2. Add vodka 1 tablespoon at a time, stirring thoroughly between additions.
3. Transfer the peach schnapps jelly/vodka mixture to a squeeze bottle.

TO MAKE THE FROSTING

1. With an electric mixer, beat shortening with the paddle attachment until fluffy.
2. With the mixer on low speed, slowly add confectioners' sugar until combined.
3. Slowly stream in cranberry juice and beat until smooth and fluffy, with no lumps or air bubbles.
4. Transfer the frosting to a piping bag.

TO MAKE THE GARNISH

1. Dice the peach into ½ inch cubes.

2. Toss peach cubes with 1 tablespoon lemon or orange juice, to prevent browning.

3. Transfer peach cubes to an airtight container lined with a paper towel. The peach cubes will keep for up to 24 hours in a refrigerator.

ASSEMBLY

1. When cupcakes are cool, core each cupcake with a small pastry tip. If you don't have a pastry tip, poke a hole in the middle of the cupcake with a narrow-bladed knife (a steak knife will do).

2. Fill cavity with the peach schnapps jelly/vodka mixture, taking care not to let it overflow.

3. Frost as desired.

4. Garnish with a peach cube.

MOJITO

Here's an amusing story. Despite starting a boozy bakery and having spent many a summer afternoon sipping on cocktails, Brooke was never a huge fan of rum and had therefore never tried a Mojito. About two years after the bakery was established, she tried a Mojito for the first time and said with no sense of irony, "It tastes just like our cupcake!"

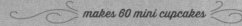
makes 60 mini cupcakes

CAKE

1²/₃ cups (208 g)	all-purpose flour
1½ teaspoons	baking powder
½ teaspoon	baking soda
¼ teaspoon	salt
1 cup (240 g)	plain yogurt
⅓ cup (70 g)	olive oil
1 cup (200 g)	granulated sugar
¼ cup (60 g)	lime juice
2 teaspoons	lime zest
2	eggs

FILLING

1 cup (230 g)	mint-infused jelly (see Infused Jelly, page 48)
¼ cup (60 g)	mint-infused rum (see Minty Rum, page 34)

FROSTING

½ cup (115 g)	shortening
1 pound	confectioners' sugar
⅓ cup (80 g)	mint-infused rum (see Minty Rum, page 34)

GARNISH

canola oil, for frying
60 uniformly sized mint leaves, approximately 1 inch long
granulated sugar

TO MAKE THE CAKE

1. Preheat the oven to 325°F. Line mini cupcake tins with paper liners.
2. Place flour, baking powder, baking soda, and salt into a separate bowl and combine. Set aside.
3. Combine yogurt, olive oil, sugar, lime juice, and lime zest in the mixing bowl of a stand mixer and beat until incorporated.
4. With the mixer running, add eggs one at a time.
5. With the mixer on low speed, slowly add the dry ingredients to the wet ingredients in the mixing bowl.
6. Mix until just combined, taking care not to overbeat.
7. Fill cupcake tins to the halfway point.
8. Bake for 10 minutes. Let cupcakes cool completely on a wire rack before filling or frosting.

TO MAKE THE FILLING

1. Whisk mint-infused jelly until smooth.
2. Add mint-infused rum, 1 tablespoon at a time, stirring thoroughly between additions.
3. Transfer the mint jelly/mint rum mixture to a squeeze bottle.

TO MAKE THE FROSTING

1. With an electric mixer, beat shortening with the paddle attachment until fluffy.
2. With the mixer on low speed, add confectioners' sugar.
3. Slowly stream in mint-infused rum and beat until smooth and fluffy, with no lumps or air bubbles.
4. Transfer the frosting to a piping bag.

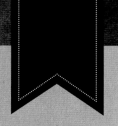

TO MAKE THE GARNISH

1. Line a plate or sheet pan with paper towels. Set aside.
2. In a medium saucepan, add canola oil halfway up the pan.
3. Heat the oil to 350°F, using a candy thermometer to check the temperature.
4. Gently fry mint leaves* until translucent, about 7 seconds.
5. Remove leaves from the oil and let drain on paper towels. Immediately sprinkle granulated sugar on the hot leaves.

ASSEMBLY

1. When cupcakes are cool, core each cupcake with a small pastry tip. If you don't have a pastry tip, poke a hole in the middle of the cupcake with a narrow-bladed knife (a steak knife will do).
2. Fill the cavity with the mint jelly/mint rum mixture, taking care not to let it overflow.
3. Frost cupcakes to your liking.
4. Garnish with a fried mint leaf.

*Frying mint is a delicate, sometimes infuriating procedure. Fry too little and you end up with a soggy mess. Fry too long and you get an oily, flavorless, brown crisp. Most mint stalks only have a handful of leaves that are the same size, and because frying dramatically shrinks the size of the leaf, a bounty of raw mint may yield only a few beautiful fried leaves. Luckily, you can use your "reject" mint for infused booze, so nothing goes to waste.

DARK 'N STORMY

The Dark 'n Stormy—the national drink of Bermuda—has the unique
distinction of being the only cocktail whose ingredients are legally
defined. The good folks at Gosling's trademarked the name, requiring
that you use their uniquely flavored dark rum when crafting a Dark
'n Stormy. So stick with the Gosling's when you're making this one,
unless you want to rename your cupcake the Overcast 'n Drizzly.

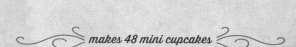

makes 48 mini cupcakes

CAKE

1	egg
1/3 cup (75 g)	sour cream
1 1/3 cups (166 g)	all-purpose flour
1 cup (200 g)	granulated sugar
3/4 teaspoon	baking soda
1/3 cup (75 g)	minced ginger
1/2 teaspoon	salt
1/2 cup	ginger beer
1/2 cup	butter, unsalted

FILLING

1 cup (230 g)	Ginger Beer Jelly (page 44)
1/4 cup (60 g)	Gosling's Dark Rum

FROSTING

1/2 cup (115 g)	shortening
1 pound	confectioners' sugar
1/3 cup (80 g)	Gosling's Dark Rum

GARNISH

lime zest

TO MAKE THE CAKE

1. Preheat the oven to 325°F. Line mini cupcake tins with paper liners.
2. In the bowl of an electric mixer, beat egg and sour cream.
3. In another bowl, combine flour, sugar, baking soda, ginger, and salt. Set aside.
4. Combine ginger beer and butter in a saucepan and heat until the butter melts.
5. With the mixer running on low speed, slowly pour in the ginger beer/butter mixture into the mixing bowl containing the egg/sour cream mixture. Beat until incorporated.
6. Slowly add the dry ingredients to the wet ingredients and beat until incorporated.
7. Fill cupcake tins two-thirds full.
8. Bake for 10 minutes. Let cupcakes cool completely on a wire rack before filling or frosting.

TO MAKE THE FILLING

1. Whisk Ginger Beer Jelly until smooth.
2. Slowly stir in Gosling's Dark Rum, 1 tablespoon at a time, stirring thoroughly between additions.
3. Transfer the Ginger Beer Jelly/rum mixture to a squeeze bottle.

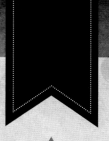

TO MAKE THE FROSTING

1. With an electric mixer, beat shortening with the paddle attachment until fluffy.

2. With the mixer on low speed, slowly add confectioners' sugar until combined.

3. Slowly stream in Gosling's Dark Rum and beat until smooth and fluffy, with no lumps or air bubbles.

4. Transfer the frosting to a piping bag.

ASSEMBLY

1. When cupcakes are cool, core each cupcake with a small pastry tip. If you don't have a pastry tip, poke a hole in the middle of the cupcake with a narrow-bladed knife (a steak knife will do).

2. Fill the cavity with the Ginger Beer Jelly/rum mixture, taking care not to let it overflow.

3. Frost to your liking.

4. Garnish with a touch of lime zest.

MAI TAI

For bartenders, Mai Tais are a red-flag drink, like Long Island Iced Teas and Mudslides. If you order one of these, a bartender will assume at least one of three things: (1) You're underage (or barely 21) and this is the only drink you've ever heard of. (2) You will be requiring frequent refills. (3) By the end of the night, you're going to be a hot mess. Please eat—and drink—responsibly.

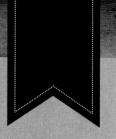

CAKE

1²/₃ cups (208 g)	all-purpose flour
1¹/₂ teaspoons	baking powder
¹/₂ teaspoon	baking soda
¹/₄ teaspoon	salt
1 cup (240 g)	plain yogurt
2¹/₂ tablespoons (40 g)	olive oil
2 tablespoons (30 g)	coconut oil
1 cup (200 g)	granulated sugar
¹/₄ cup (60 g)	orange juice
2 teaspoons	orange zest
2	eggs

FILLING

1 cup (230 g)	Pineapple Sauce (page 52)
¹/₄ cup (60 g)	golden rum

FROSTING

1 stick (115 g)	butter, unsalted
1 pound	confectioners' sugar
¹/₄ cup (60 g)	coconut rum
4 teaspoons (20 g)	grenadine*

GARNISH

cherry (optional)

---

*Now would be a great time to check out the recipe for Grenadine on page 297. Just sayin'.

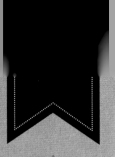

TO MAKE THE CAKE

1. Preheat the oven to 325°F. Line mini cupcake tins with paper liners.
2. Place flour, baking powder, baking soda, and salt in a bowl and combine. Set aside.
3. Combine yogurt, olive oil, coconut oil, sugar, orange juice, and orange zest in the bowl of a stand mixer and beat until incorporated.
4. With the mixer running, add eggs one at a time.
5. With the mixer on low speed, slowly add the dry ingredients to the wet ingredients in the mixing bowl.
6. Mix until just combined, taking care not to overbeat.
7. Fill cupcake tins to the halfway point.
8. Bake for 10 minutes. Let cupcakes cool completely on a wire rack before filling or frosting.

TO MAKE THE FILLING

1. Whisk the Pineapple Sauce until smooth.
2. Add golden rum 1 tablespoon at a time, stirring thoroughly between additions.
3. Transfer the Pineapple Sauce/rum mixture to a squeeze bottle.

TO MAKE THE FROSTING

1. With an electric mixer, beat butter with the paddle attachment until fluffy.
2. With the mixer on low speed, slowly add confectioners' sugar until combined.
3. Slowly stream in coconut rum and grenadine, and beat until smooth and fluffy, with no lumps or air bubbles.
4. Transfer the frosting to a piping bag.

ASSEMBLY

1. When cupcakes are cool, core each cupcake with a small pastry tip. If you don't have a pastry tip, poke a hole in the middle of the cupcake with a narrow-bladed knife (a steak knife will do).
2. Fill the cavity with the Pineapple Sauce/golden rum mixture, taking care not to let it overflow.
3. Frost as desired.
4. Garnish with a cherry (optional).

STRAWBERRY DAIQUIRI

When we first figured out this cupcake, a lifetime ago—which is what it feels like—we actually jumped up and down for joy, it was so good. One of our best sellers during our catering days, it was eventually abandoned to make room for other rummy flavors. Who knows? Maybe we will meet again.

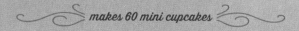
makes 60 mini cupcakes

CAKE

1²⁄₃ cups (208 g)	all-purpose flour
1 ½ teaspoons	baking powder
½ teaspoon	baking soda
¼ teaspoon	salt
1 cup (240 g)	plain yogurt
⅓ cup (70 g)	olive oil
1 cup (200 g)	granulated sugar
¼ cup (60 g)	strawberry juice, reserved from strawberry puree (see Fruit Puree, page 51)
2	eggs

FILLING

1 cup (230 g)	strawberry puree with rum (see Fruit Puree, page 51)
¼ cup (60 g)	white rum

FROSTING

½ cup (115 g)	shortening
1 pound	confectioners' sugar
⅓ cup (80 g)	light rum

GARNISH

lime zest

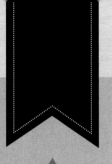

TO MAKE THE CAKE

1. Preheat the oven to 325°F. Line mini cupcake tins with paper liners.

2. Place flour, baking powder, baking soda, and salt in a separate bowl and combine. Set aside.

3. Combine yogurt, olive oil sugar, and strawberry juice into the mixing bowl of a stand mixer and beat until incorporated.

4. With the mixer running, add eggs one at a time.

5. With the mixer on low speed, slowly add the dry ingredients to the wet ingredients in the mixing bowl.

6. Mix until just combined, taking care not to overbeat.

7. Fill cupcake tins to the halfway point.

8. Bake for 10 minutes. Let cupcakes cool completely on a wire rack before filling and frosting.

TO MAKE THE FILLING

1. Whisk the strawberry puree until smooth.

2. Add white rum 1 tablespoon at a time, stirring thoroughly after each addition.

3. Transfer the strawberry puree/rum mixture to a squeeze bottle.

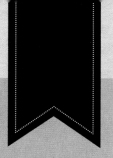

TO MAKE THE FROSTING

1. With an electric mixer, beat shortening with the paddle attachment until fluffy.

2. With the mixer on low speed, slowly add confectioners' sugar until combined.

3. Slowly stream in white rum and beat until smooth and fluffy, with no lumps or air bubbles.

4. Transfer the frosting to a piping bag.

ASSEMBLY

1. When cupcakes are cool, core each cupcake with a small pastry tip. If you don't have a pastry tip, poke a hole in the middle of the cupcake with a narrow-bladed knife (a steak knife will do).

2. Fill the cavity with the strawberry puree/rum mixture, taking care not to let it overflow.

3. Frost cupcakes to your liking.

4. Sprinkle each cupcake with a tiny pinch of lime zest.

HOT BUTTERED RUM

As a cocktail, melted butter and rum is a pretty revolting concept, but as a cupcake it's amazing. The key to this cupcake is the brown butter, which brings incredible richness to the frosting. Brown butter is as easy to make as it is to screw up, but when you get it right it is so worth all of the burned butter, the smoky kitchen, and the strings of expletives.

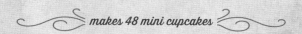

makes 48 mini cupcakes

CAKE

1	egg
⅓ cup (75 g)	sour cream
1⅓ cups (166 g)	all-purpose flour
1 cup (200 g)	sugar
¾ teaspoon	baking soda
½ teaspoon	cinnamon
½ teaspoon	nutmeg
½ teaspoon	salt
½ cup (115 g)	water
1 stick (115 g)	butter, unsalted

FILLING

1 cup (230 g)	Caramel Sauce, made with rum (page 53)

FROSTING

1 stick (115 g)	butter, unsalted
1 pound	confectioners' sugar
⅓ cup (80 g)	dark rum

GARNISH

brown sugar

TO MAKE THE CAKE

1. Preheat the oven to 325°F. Line mini cupcake tins with paper liners.
2. In the bowl of an electric mixer, beat egg and sour cream. Set aside.
3. In another bowl, combine flour, sugar, baking soda, cinnamon, nutmeg, and salt. Set aside.
4. Combine water and butter in a saucepan and heat until the butter melts.
5. Remove from heat. With the mixer on low speed, slowly pour the hot water/butter mixture into the mixing bowl containing the egg/sour cream mixture. Beat until incorporated.
6. Slowly add the dry ingredients to the wet ingredients and beat until incorporated.
7. Fill cupcake tins two-thirds full.
8. Bake for 10 minutes. Let cupcakes cool completely on a wire rack before filling or frosting.

TO MAKE THE FROSTING

The Day Before

1. Heat butter in a saucepan over low heat until it is fully melted.
2. Turn the heat up to medium-high, keeping a close eye on the butter. Stir constantly, taking care to scrape the bottom of the pan.
3. Remove the pan from the heat once the butter begins to take on an amber color and smell faintly nutty, and little flecks of browned butter are visible. Keep a close watch over your butter at this point. The difference between browned butter and burnt butter is a matter of seconds.
4. Transfer butter to a heat-proof container, taking care to scrape every last fleck of browned goodness out of the pan.
5. Cool in the refrigerator.

The Day Of

1. Allow browned butter to soften, and then combine with confectioners' sugar in a standing mixer on low speed.

2. Slowly add dark rum and beat until fluffy.

3. Transfer the frosting to a piping bag.

▲
ASSEMBLY
▼

1. When cupcakes are cool, core each cupcake with a small pastry tip. If you don't have a pastry tip, poke a hole in the middle of the cupcake with a narrow-bladed knife (a steak knife will do).

2. Fill each cavity with rummy caramel, taking care not to let it overflow.

3. Frost to your liking.

4. Garnish with a sprinkle of brown sugar.

BREAKFAST, BITCH*

While most of our cupcakes are derived from cocktails, we take particular pride in our conceptual cupcakes. The Breakfast, Bitch cupcake was designed to incorporate all the flavors of breakfast in a single, delicious, boozy bite.

*The name of this cupcake comes from the 2008 song "Breakfast" by LeLe.

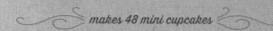
makes 48 mini cupcakes

CAKE

1 stick (115 g)	butter, unsalted
1 cup (115 g)	water
1	egg
1/3 cup (75 g)	sour cream
1 1/3 cups (166 g)	all-purpose flour
1 cup (200 g)	granulated sugar
3/4 teaspoon	baking soda
3/4 teaspoon	cinnamon
1/2 teaspoon	salt
3/4 teaspoon	vanilla

FILLING

1 cup (230 g)	White Chocolate Ganache, made with rum (page 39)

FROSTING

1 stick (115 g)	butter, unsalted
1 pound	confectioners' sugar
1/3 cup (80 g)	coffee liqueur

GARNISH

bacon*

---

* Feel free to prepare the bacon however you like, but we recommend laying it flat on a cookie sheet and baking it in the oven, with the cupcakes, so the bacon-y aroma surrounds the baking cakes. Depending on the thickness of the bacon, you may need to cook it longer than the 10 minutes it takes to bake the cupcakes. Just keep an eye on it and make sure it gets nice and crispy. Drain off all the excess oil and let the bacon slices cool before garnishing.

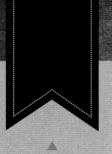

TO MAKE THE CAKE

1. Heat butter in a saucepan over low heat until it is fully melted.

2. Turn heat up to medium, keeping a close eye on the butter. Stir constantly, taking care to scrape the bottom of the pan.

3. Remove the pan from heat once the butter begins to take on an amber color and smell faintly nutty, and little flecks of browned butter are visible.

4. Add water, and return to stove.

5. Cook on medium heat for 1 minute to allow water to warm; prevent butter from cooling too much.

6. Remove from heat.

7. Preheat the oven to 325°F. Line mini cupcake tins with paper liners.

8. In the bowl of an electric mixer, beat egg and sour cream.

9. In another bowl, combine flour, sugar, baking soda, cinnamon, and salt. Set aside.

10. With the mixer running on low, slowly pour the water and browned butter mixture into the mixer bowl. Beat until incorporated.

11. Slowly add the dry ingredients to the wet ingredients and beat until incorporated.

12. Add vanilla.

13. Fill cupcake tins two-thirds full.

14. Bake for 10 minutes. Let cupcakes cool completely on a wire rack before filling or frosting.

TO MAKE THE FROSTING

1. With an electric mixer, beat butter with the paddle attachment until fluffy.

2. With the mixer on low speed, slowly add confectioners' sugar until combined.

3. Add coffee liqueur and beat until smooth and fluffy. Slowly stream in coffee liqueur and beat until smooth and fluffy, with no lumps or air bubbles.

4. Transfer the frosting to a piping bag.

ASSEMBLY

1. When cupcakes are cool, core each cupcake with a small pastry tip. If you don't have a pastry tip, poke a hole in the middle of the cupcake with a narrow-bladed knife (a steak knife will do).

2. Fill the cavity with the rummy White Chocolate Ganache, taking care not to let it overflow.

3. Frost cupcakes to your liking.

4. Garnish with a bit of bacon slice.

MONKEY BUSINESS

As you can well imagine, our families are pretty excited about all things Prohibition Bakery, and they have been from the start. Leslie's dad particularly loved being a tester for new cupcake flavors during the early days of the bakery and was put to work whenever possible. This was his absolute favorite.

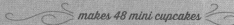

CAKE

1 stick (115 g)	butter, melted
1½ cups (187 g)	all-purpose flour
¾ cup (150 g)	granulated sugar
1 teaspoon	baking powder
1 teaspoon	baking soda
½ teaspoon	salt
½ teaspoon	cinnamon
3	brown bananas*
1	egg

FILLING

1 cup (230 g)	Bittersweet Chocolate Ganache, made with rum[†] (page 38)

FROSTING

2 ounces	milk chocolate
1 stick (115 g)	butter, unsalted
1 pound	confectioners' sugar
⅓ cup (80 g)	cold brewed coffee

GARNISH

chocolate shavings (optional)

---

*The browner the bananas, the more of their complex carbohydrates have been converted to simple sugars. Bananas become browned over time, when the complex carbohydrates convert to simple sugars. In other words, the darker the banana, the sweeter the banana. As the carbohydrates break down, the banana becomes moist and soft, and thus better for baking. If you can't find brown bananas, put ripe ones on a sheet pan in a 300°F oven for 35 minutes or in a sealed paper bag overnight.

† A gold or dark rum would be best.

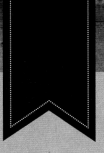

TO MAKE THE CAKE

1. Preheat the oven to 325°F. Line mini cupcake tins with paper liners.
2. Melt butter in a saucepan or in microwave on low heat. Put to the side to cool slightly.
3. Combine flour, sugar, baking powder, baking soda, salt, and cinnamon in a separate bowl. Set aside.
4. Peel the bananas and place them in a mixing bowl. Beat until relatively smooth.
5. While the mixer is running, add egg and mix until completely combined.
6. Slowly add melted butter.
7. Slowly add the dry ingredients to the banana mixture while mixing at low speed.
8. Fill cupcake tins two-thirds full.
9. Bake for 10 minutes. Let cupcakes cool completely on a wire rack before filling or frosting.

TO MAKE THE FROSTING

1. In a small saucepan, melt chocolate over low heat. You can also microwave it on medium for 15-second intervals, mixing in between intervals, until completely smooth. It will likely take a total of 1–1½ minutes of microwaving.
2. With an electric mixer, beat butter with the paddle attachment until fluffy.
3. With the mixer on low speed, slowly add confectioners' sugar until combined.
4. Slowly stream in cold coffee and beat until smooth and fluffy, with no lumps or air bubbles.
5. Add melted chocolate slowly and beat until smooth and fluffy, with no lumps or air bubbles.
6. Transfer the frosting to a piping bag.

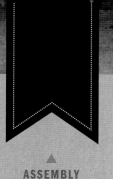

ASSEMBLY

1. When cupcakes are cool, core each cupcake with a small pastry tip. If you don't have a pastry tip, poke a hole in the middle of the cupcake with a narrow-bladed knife (a steak knife will do).

2. Fill the cavity with Bittersweet Chocolate Ganache made with rum, taking care not to let it overflow.

3. Frost cupcakes to your liking.

4. Garnish with chocolate shavings, if desired.

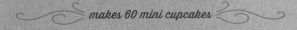
makes 60 mini cupcakes

CAKE

1 ²/₃ cups (208 g)	all-purpose flour
1¹/₂ teaspoons	baking powder
¹/₂ teaspoon	baking soda
¹/₄ teaspoon	salt
1 cup (240 g)	plain yogurt
2¹/₂ tablespoons (40 g)	olive oil
2 tablespoons (30 g)	coconut oil
1 cup (200 g)	granulated sugar
¹/₄ cup (60 g)	pineapple juice
2	eggs

FILLING

1 cup (115 g)	coconut cream (like Coco Lopez)
¹/₄ cup (60 g)	dark rum

FROSTING

1 cup (115 g)	shortening
1 pound	confectioners' sugar
¹/₃ cup (80 g)	pineapple juice

GARNISH

1 cup	shredded or flaked coconut

PIÑA COLADA

Although this is perhaps one of the most obvious cocktails-turned-cupcakes, we somehow didn't put it on the menu until the summer of 2014. Right around that time, we received the honor of being named two of "Zagat's 30 under 30" for 2014. The next thing you know, the Piña Colada cupcakes were famous for being featured in Zagat.

TO MAKE THE CAKE

1. Preheat the oven to 325°F. Line mini cupcake tins with paper liners.

2. Place flour, baking powder, baking soda, and salt in a separate bowl and combine. Set aside.

3. Combine yogurt, olive oil, coconut oil, sugar, and pineapple juice into the mixing bowl of a stand mixer and beat until incorporated.

4. With the mixer running, add eggs one at a time.

5. With the mixer on low speed, slowly add the dry ingredients to the wet ingredients in the mixing bowl.

6. Mix until just combined, taking care not to overbeat.

7. Fill cupcake tins to the halfway point.

8. Bake for 10 minutes. Let cupcakes cool completely on a wire rack before filling or frosting.

TO MAKE THE FILLING

1. Scoop coconut cream from can, taking care to avoid the coconut oil (you can use this in the cake), and use only the thicker cream.

2. Whisk in dark rum 1 tablespoon at a time, stirring thoroughly after each addition.

3. Transfer the coconut cream/rum mixture to a squeeze bottle.

TO MAKE THE FROSTING

1. With an electric mixer, beat shortening with the paddle attachment until fluffy.

2. With the mixer on low speed, slowly add confectioners' sugar until incorporated.

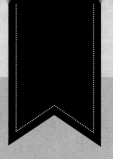

3. While the mixer is running, stream in pineapple juice. Slowly stream in pineapple juice and beat until smooth and fluffy, with no lumps or air bubbles.

4. Transfer the frosting to a piping bag.

▲ TO MAKE THE GARNISH ▼

1. Preheat the oven to 325°F.

2. Spread coconut on a sheet pan in a single layer.

3. Bake until golden brown.*

▲ ASSEMBLY ▼

1. When cupcakes are cool, core each cupcake with a small pastry tip. If you don't have a pastry tip, poke a hole in the middle of the cupcake with a narrow-bladed knife (a steak knife will do).

2. Fill the cavity with the coconut cream/rum mixture, taking care not to let it overflow.

3. Frost cupcakes to your liking.

4. Garnish with toasted coconut.

*Coconut can go from golden brown to burned in a matter of seconds, so take care to watch your coconut while it's toasting. If you have an oven that bakes unevenly, be particularly watchful— the coconut may burn on the outside of the pan before the inside is even golden, or vice versa. Just give the coconut a quick stir if you notice one section is browning more quickly than another.

KOKOLOKO

This cupcake exists for no other reason than that coconut and chocolate are a fantastic combination. As boozy bakers, we needed to incorporate booze somehow, and dark rum seemed like the best choice to complement both the coconut and the chocolate.

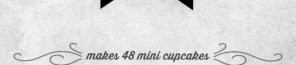

CAKE

1	egg
⅓ cup (75 g)	sour cream
1 cup (125 g)	all-purpose flour
1 cup (200 g)	granulated sugar
¾ teaspoon	baking soda
½ teaspoon	salt
½ cup (115 g)	plain coconut water
1 stick (115 g)	butter, unsalted
⅓ cup (45 g)	dark cocoa powder

FILLING

1 cup (230 g)	Bittersweet Chocolate Ganache, made with coconut rum (page 38)

FROSTING

1 stick (115 g)	butter, unsalted
1 pound	confectioners' sugar
⅓ cup (80 g)	dark rum

GARNISH

1 cup (230 g)	toasted coconut flakes

TO MAKE THE CAKE

1. Preheat the oven to 325°F. Line mini cupcake tins with paper liners.
2. In the bowl of an electric mixer, beat egg and sour cream.
3. In another bowl, combine flour, sugar, baking soda, and salt. Set aside.
4. Combine coconut water and butter in a saucepan and heat until butter melts.
5. Remove from heat and whisk in cocoa powder. With the mixer running, slowly pour the hot cocoa/butter mixture into the mixer bowl. Beat until incorporated.
6. Slowly add the dry ingredients to the wet ingredients and beat until incorporated.
7. Fill cupcake tins two-thirds full.
8. Bake for 10 minutes. Let cupcakes cool completely on a wire rack before filling or frosting.

TO MAKE THE FROSTING

1. With an electric mixer, beat butter with the paddle attachment until fluffy.

2. With the mixer on low speed, slowly add confectioners' sugar until incorporated.

3. Slowly stream in dark rum and beat until smooth and fluffy, with no lumps or air bubbles.

4. Transfer the frosting to a piping bag.

TO MAKE THE GARNISH

1. Preheat the oven to 325°F.

2. Spread coconut on a sheet pan in a single layer.

3. Bake until golden brown.

ASSEMBLY

1. When cupcakes are cool, core each cupcake with a small pastry tip. If you don't have a pastry tip, poke a hole in the middle of the cupcake with a narrow-bladed knife (a steak knife will do).

2. Fill the cavity with Bittersweet Chocolate Ganache with coconut rum, taking care not to let it overflow.

3. Frost cupcakes to your liking.

4. Garnish with toasted coconut.

This is Leslie's go-to drink, so of course it was one of the cupcakes we had the most difficulty conceptualizing. The key is the boozy cherry on top, which you'll need to make at least a day ahead. You can alter many aspects of this cupcake to suit your tastes (rye anyone?), but for the love of God, don't leave off the cherry!

OLD FASHIONED

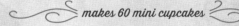

makes 60 mini cupcakes

CAKE

1²⁄₃ cups (208 g)	all-purpose flour
1¹⁄₂ teaspoons	baking powder
¹⁄₂ teaspoon	baking soda
¹⁄₄ teaspoon	salt
1 cup (240 g)	plain yogurt
¹⁄₃ cup (70 g)	olive oil
1 cup (200 g)	granulated sugar
¹⁄₄ cup (60 g)	orange juice
2 teaspoons	orange zest
2	eggs

FILLING

1 cup (230 g)	Cherry Jelly (p. 50)
¹⁄₄ cup (60 g)	bourbon

FROSTING

¹⁄₂ cup (115 g)	shortening
1 pound	confectioners' sugar
¹⁄₃ cup (80 g)	bourbon
6–8 dashes	aromatic bitters

GARNISH

¹⁄₂ cup (115 g)	dried cherries
¹⁄₂ cup (115 g)	bourbon

TO MAKE THE CAKE

1. Preheat the oven to 325°F. Line mini cupcake tins with paper liners.
2. Place flour, baking powder, baking soda, and salt in a separate bowl and combine. Set aside.
3. Combine yogurt, olive oil, sugar, orange juice, and orange zest in the mixing bowl of a stand mixer and beat until incorporated.
4. With the mixer running, add eggs one at a time.
5. With the mixer on low speed, slowly add the dry ingredients to the wet ingredients. Mix until just combined, taking care not to overbeat.
6. Fill cupcake tins to the halfway point.
7. Bake for 10 minutes. Let cupcakes cool completely on a wire rack before filling or frosting.

TO MAKE THE FILLING

1. Whisk the Cherry Jelly until smooth.
2. Add bourbon 1 tablespoon at a time, stirring thoroughly between additions.
3. Transfer the Cherry Jelly/bourbon mixture to a squeeze bottle.

TO MAKE THE FROSTING

1. With an electric mixer, beat shortening with the paddle attachment until fluffy.
2. With the mixer on low speed, slowly add confectioners' sugar until combined.
3. While the mixer is running, slowly stream in bourbon and bitters and beat until smooth and fluffy, with no lumps or air bubbles.
4. Transfer the frosting to a piping bag.

TO MAKE THE GARNISH

1. Place cherries in an airtight container.

2. Fill the container with bourbon until cherries are completely covered.

3. Let sit for at least 24 hours, preferably 3–5 days.

4. Remove cherries from the bourbon and let dry on a paper towel for at least 2–3 hours. Use your new cherry-infused bourbon to make a nice Old Fashioned cocktail* to fill you with anticipation for Old Fashioned cupcakes.

5. Store cherries in a clean, airtight container. They will keep unrefrigerated for up to two weeks.

ASSEMBLY

1. When cupcakes are cool, core each cupcake with a small pastry tip. If you don't have a pastry tip, poke a hole in the middle of the cupcake with a narrow-bladed knife (a steak knife will do).

2. Fill the cavity with the Cherry Jelly/bourbon mixture, taking care not to let it overflow.

3. Frost cupcakes to your liking.

4. Top with a bourbon cherry.

---

*Mixing drinking and baking is only recommended for those with considerable experience in both areas!

This Prohibition-era cocktail had been all but forgot until its revival in recent years. It is often advertise a "female-friendly" whiskey drink, a characterizati that is not only outdated and patronizing but also p confusing. We're not sure what is so lady-friendly a rye, ginger, and bitters, but either way, everyone c and should enjoy this cocktail and cupcake.

HORSEFEATHERS

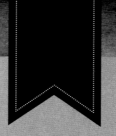

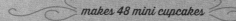
makes 48 mini cupcakes

CAKE

1	egg
1/3 cup (75 g)	sour cream
1 1/3 cups (166 g)	all-purpose flour
1 cup (200 g)	granulated sugar
3/4 teaspoon	baking soda
1/2 teaspoon	salt
1/2 cup (115 g)	ginger beer
1 stick (115 g)	butter
1/4 cup (60 g)	fresh ginger, finely grated

FILLING

1 cup (230 g)	Ginger Beer Jelly (page 44)
1/3 cup (80 g)	rye whiskey

FROSTING

1/2 cup (115 g)	shortening
1 pound	confectioners' sugar
1/3 cup (80 g)	rye whiskey
6 heavy dashes	aromatic bitters

GARNISH

lemon zest

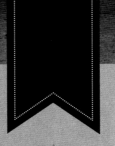

TO MAKE THE CAKE

1. Preheat the oven to 325°F. Line mini cupcake tins with paper liners.
2. In the bowl of an electric mixer, beat egg and sour cream.
3. In another bowl, combine flour, sugar, baking soda, and salt. Set aside.
4. Combine ginger beer and butter in a saucepan, and heat until the butter melts.
5. With the mixer running on low speed, slowly pour the hot ginger beer/butter mixture into the mixer bowl with the egg/sour cream mixture. Beat until incorporated.
6. Slowly add the dry ingredients to the wet ingredients and beat thoroughly.
7. Add grated ginger, and beat until incorporated.
8. Fill cupcake tins two-thirds full.
9. Bake for 10 minutes. Let cupcakes cool completely on a wire rack before filling or frosting.

TO MAKE THE FILLING

1. Whisk Ginger Beer Jelly until smooth.
2. Add whiskey 1 tablespoon at a time, stirring thoroughly between each addition.
3. Transfer to a squeeze bottle.

TO MAKE THE FROSTING

1. With an electric mixer, beat shortening with the paddle attachment until fluffy.

2. With the mixer on low speed, slowly add confectioners' sugar until combined.

3. Slowly stream in rye and bitters and beat until smooth and fluffy, with no lumps or air bubbles.

4. Transfer the frosting to a piping bag.

ASSEMBLY

1. When cupcakes are cool, core each cupcake with a small pastry tip. If you don't have a pastry tip, poke a hole in the middle of the cupcake with a narrow-bladed knife (a steak knife will do).

2. Fill the cavity with the rye whiskey/Ginger Beer Jelly mixture, taking care not to let it overflow.

3. Frost cupcakes to your liking.

4. Garnish with a tiny pinch of lemon zest (a little goes a long way).

MACALLAN

We partnered with Macallan in our first year at the bakery and wanted to make a cupcake that reflected the nuances of a Macallan 12. After tasting and reading about the spirit, we found hints of orange, fig, oak, and nuts, so we simply incorporated those flavors into the cupcake and adjusted their ratios from prototype to prototype until we found a balance. Try this cupcake, and you'll see what we mean.

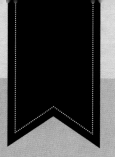

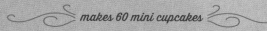

makes 60 mini cupcakes

CAKE

1 2/3 cups (208 g)	all-purpose flour
1 1/2 teaspoons	baking powder
1/2 teaspoon	baking soda
1/4 teaspoon	salt
1 cup (240 g)	yogurt
1/3 cup (70 g)	olive oil
1 cup (200 g)	granulated sugar
1/4 cup (60 g)	orange juice
1/3 cup (80 g)	Whiskey Fig Jam (page 41)
1 teaspoon	orange zest
2	eggs

FILLING

1 cup (230 g)	Whiskey Fig Jam (page 41)
1/4 cup (60 g)	Macallan 12*

FROSTING

2 cups (115 g)	shortening
1 pound	confectioners' sugar
1/3 cup (80 g)	Macallan 12
3 tablespoons (50 g)	Whiskey Fig Jam (page 41)
1/4 cup	finely chopped walnuts

GARNISH

milk chocolate curl

---

*If you follow Scotch, you'll know that in 2012 Macallan started a bit of a scandal when they announced they would start bottling by color, not year, which is contrary to all of Scotch culture. We can't attest to the flavor of any of their new bottlings, but the Macallan 12 is perfect for this cupcake.

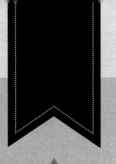

TO MAKE THE CAKE

1. Preheat the oven to 325°F. Line mini cupcake tins with paper liners.
2. Place flour, baking powder, baking soda, and salt in a bowl, and combine. Set aside.
3. Combine yogurt, olive oil, sugar, orange juice, Whiskey Fig Jam, and orange zest in the mixing bowl of a stand mixer, and beat until incorporated.
4. With the mixer running, add eggs one at a time.
5. With the mixer on low speed, slowly add the dry ingredients to the wet ingredients in the mixing bowl.
6. Mix until just combined, taking care not to overbeat.
7. Fill cupcake tins to the halfway point.
8. Bake for 10 minutes. Let cupcakes cool completely on a wire rack before filling or frosting.

TO MAKE THE FILLING

1. Whisk the Whiskey Fig Jam until smooth.
2. Add in Macallan 1 tablespoon at a time, stirring thoroughly after each addition.
3. Transfer the Whiskey Fig Jam/Macallan mixture to a squeeze bottle.

TO MAKE THE FROSTING

1. With an electric mixer, beat shortening with the paddle attachment until fluffy.

2. With the mixer on low speed, slowly add confectioners' sugar until combined.

3. Slowly stream in Macallan 12 and beat until smooth and fluffy, with no lumps or air bubbles.

4. Add Whiskey Fig Jam and walnuts and beat until incorporated.

5. Transfer the frosting to a piping bag.

ASSEMBLY

1. When cupcakes are cool, core each cupcake with a small pastry tip. If you don't have a pastry tip, poke a hole in the middle of the cupcake with a narrow-bladed knife (a steak knife will do).

2. Fill the cavity with the Whiskey Fig Jam/Macallan mixture, taking care not to let it overflow.

3. Frost cupcakes as desired.

4. Using a peeler, create small curls of milk chocolate and top each cupcake with a curl.

MEXICAN HOT CHOCOLATE

The last few years have seen a surge in the popularity of spicy chocolate. But do you know what's even better than spicy chocolate? Boozy spicy chocolate. Make these cupcakes for the next Cinco de Mayo and serve them along with Margarita cupcakes (page 186) for a little something different.

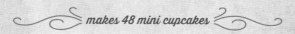 *makes 48 mini cupcakes*

CAKE

1	egg
⅓ cup (75 g)	sour cream
1 cup (125 g)	all-purpose flour
1 cup (200 g)	granulated sugar
¾ teaspoon	baking soda
1 teaspoon	ground cinnamon
½ teaspoon	salt
½ cup (115 g)	stout
1 stick (115 g)	butter
⅓ cup (45 g)	cocoa powder
½ teaspoon	vanilla

CHILE DE ÁRBOL–INFUSED CREAM

3	dried árbol chiles
2¼ cups (500 g)	heavy cream

FILLING

1 cup (230 g)	Bittersweet Chocolate Ganache (page 38), made with chile de árbol–infused whiskey (see Spicy Scotch, page 35)*

FROSTING

1 cup (230 g)	chile de árbol cream
16 ounces (454 g)	bittersweet chocolate, finely chopped

GARNISH

ground cinnamon, for dusting

TO MAKE THE CAKE

1. Preheat the oven to 325°F. Line mini cupcake tins with paper liners.

2. In the bowl of an electric mixer, beat egg and sour cream.

3. In another bowl, combine flour, sugar, baking soda, cinnamon, and salt. Set aside.

4. Combine stout and butter in a saucepan and heat until the butter melts.

5. Remove from heat and whisk in cocoa powder. While the mixer is running on low, slowly pour the hot cocoa/butter mixture in the mixing bowl containing the egg/sour cream mixture. Mix until incorporated.

6. With the mixer on low, slowly add the dry ingredients to the wet ingredients and beat until incorporated.

7. Add vanilla and mix thoroughly.

8. Fill cupcake tins two-thirds full.

9. Bake for 10 minutes. Let cupcakes cool completely on a wire rack before filling or frosting.

TO MAKE THE CHILE DE ÁRBOL–INFUSED CREAM FOR GANACHE

1. In a saucepan, crush dried chiles de árbol. Pour the cream over the chiles.

2. Place the saucepan over medium-low heat and simmer, taking care not to scald the mixture.

3. Reduce by half.

4. Remove from heat and let cool.

5. When the infused cream is cool, strain and discard chiles.

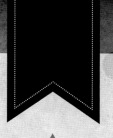

TO MAKE THE FROSTING

1. In the saucepan, reheat the strained chile de árbol cream until just bubbling, taking care not to scald.

2. Remove cream from heat, and pour over bittersweet chocolate. Let the mixture sit for at least 1 minute, then gently stir until incorporated. Let ganache come to room temperature before moving on to step 3.

3. When you are ready to frost the cupcakes, beat the room-temperature chile de árbol-infused bittersweet chocolate ganache on high speed in a stand mixer with a paddle attachment until fluffy and soft.

4. Transfer the frosting to a piping bag.

ASSEMBLY

1. When cupcakes are cool, core each cupcake with a small pastry tip. If you don't have a pastry tip, poke a hole in the middle of the cupcake with a narrow-bladed knife (a steak knife will do).

2. Fill the cavity with the chile de árbol-infused whiskey Bittersweet Chocolate Ganache,* taking care not to let it overflow.

3. Frost cupcakes to your liking.

4. Dust with cinnamon.

---

*You may want to eat the entire bowl of spicy ganache like a big bowl of pudding. Show a little restraint, as that chile de árbol sneaks up on you.

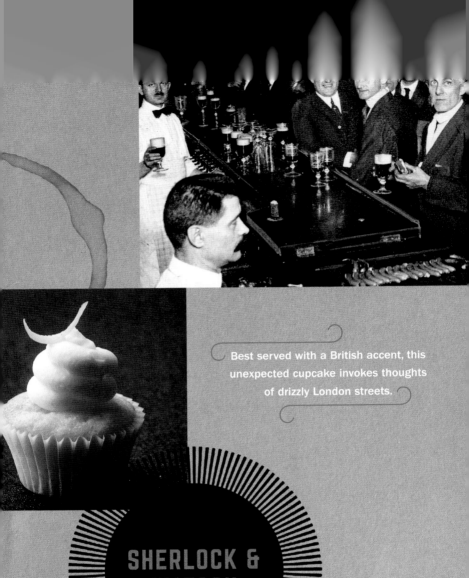

Best served with a British accent, this unexpected cupcake invokes thoughts of drizzly London streets.

SHERLOCK & WATSON

OHIBITION BAKE

EST. 2011

I like my cupcakes like I like my men, rich + full of booze.

↓ BOOZY CUPCAKES ↓

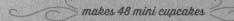
makes 48 mini cupcakes

CAKE

1	egg
⅓ cup (75 g)	sour cream
1⅓ cups (166 g)	all-purpose flour
1 cup (200 g)	granulated sugar
¾ teaspoon	baking soda
1 teaspoon	lemon zest
1 teaspoon	ground cardamom
½ teaspoon	salt
½ cup (115 g)	strong brewed Earl Grey tea*
1 stick (115 g)	butter

FILLING

1 cup (230 g)	Earl Grey-infused jelly (see Infused Jelly, page 48)
¼ cup (60 g)	Highland Scotch

FROSTING

1 stick (115 g)	butter, unsalted
1 pound	confectioners' sugar
⅓ cup (80 g)	Highland Scotch

GARNISH

lemon zest

---

*Any black tea should do. Just make sure to make it stronger than you would normally drink it. You really want the flavor to come through in the cake.

TO MAKE THE CAKE

1. Preheat the oven to 325°F. Line mini cupcake tins with paper liners.

2. In the bowl of an electric mixer, beat egg and sour cream.

3. In another bowl, combine flour, sugar, baking soda, lemon zest, cardamom, and salt. Set aside.

4. Combine tea and butter in a small saucepan and heat until the butter melts.

5. With the mixer on low speed, slowly pour the hot tea/butter mixture into the mixer bowl containing the egg/sour cream mixture. Beat until incorporated.

6. Slowly add the dry ingredients to the wet ingredients and beat until incorporated.

7. Fill cupcake tins two-thirds full.

8. Bake for 10 minutes. Let cupcakes cool completely on a wire rack before filling or frosting.

TO MAKE THE FILLING

1. Whisk the Earl Grey Jelly until smooth.

2. Add in Highland Scotch 1 tablespoon at a time, stirring thorougly after each addition.

3. Transfer the Earl Grey-infused jelly/Scotch mixture to a squeeze bottle.

TO MAKE THE FROSTING

1. With an electric mixer, beat butter with the paddle attachment until fluffy.

2. With the mixer on low speed, slowly add confectioners' sugar until combined.

3. Slowly stream in Scotch and beat until smooth and fluffy, with no lumps or air bubbles.

4. Transfer the frosting to a piping bag.

ASSEMBLY

1. When cupcakes are cool, core each cupcake with a small pastry tip. If you don't have a pastry tip, poke a hole in the middle of the cupcake with a narrow-bladed knife (a steak knife will do).

2. Fill the cavity with the Earl Grey-infused jelly/Scotch mixture, taking care not to let it overflow.

3. Frost cupcakes to your liking.

4. Garnish with a touch of lemon zest.

THE SMOKING GUN

In this recipe for a rare, filling-less boozy cupcake, the seemingly opposite flavors of Fernet-Branca and peaty Scotch come together in a surprisingly delicious—and manly—cupcake. Peaty Scotch makes for one of the best frostings we've ever created, but few other flavors can compete with its overwhelming flavor. One-of-a-kind, herbaceous Fernet-Branca stands up to the challenge.

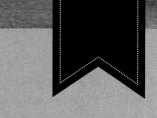

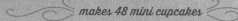

makes 48 mini cupcakes

CAKE

1	egg
⅓ cup (75 g)	sour cream
1 cup (125 g)	all-purpose flour
1 cup (200 g)	granulated sugar
¾ teaspoon	baking soda
⅓ cup (45 g)	ground graham crackers
½ teaspoon	salt
¾ cup (180 g)	Fernet-Branca*
1 stick (115 g)	butter, unsalted

FROSTING

1 stick (115 g)	butter, unsalted
1 pound	confectioners' sugar
⅓ cup (80 g)	peaty Scotch, such as Laphroaig
4 dashes	Angostura bitters

GARNISH

brown sugar cubes, broken into chunks

---

*Fernet-Branca, created in Italy in the 1800s, is now the drink of choice of mustachioed hipsters the world over. Because it is essentially a sugar-free bitters, containing 20 to 40 different herbs and spices, Fernet-Branca continued to be sold throughout Prohibition in America for its "medicinal qualities." The drink's nuances can be an acquired taste.

143

TO MAKE THE CAKE

1. Preheat the oven to 325°F. Line mini cupcake tins with paper liners.

2. In the bowl of an electric mixer, beat egg and sour cream.

3. In another bowl, combine flour, sugar, baking soda, ground graham crackers, and salt. Set aside.

4. Combine Fernet-Branca and butter in a saucepan, and heat until the butter melts.

5. With the mixer on low speed, slowly pour the hot Fernet-Branca/butter mixture into the mixer bowl containing the egg/sour cream mixture. Beat until incorporated.

6. Slowly add the dry ingredients to the wet ingredients and beat until incorporated.

7. Fill cupcake tins two-thirds full.

8. Bake for 10 minutes. Let cupcakes cool completely on a wire rack before filling or frosting.

TO MAKE THE FROSTING

1. With an electric mixer, beat butter with the paddle attachment until fluffy.
2. With the mixer on low speed, slowly add confectioners' sugar until combined.
3. Slowly stream in Scotch and bitters and beat until smooth and fluffy, with no lumps or air bubbles.
4. Transfer the frosting to a piping bag.

ASSEMBLY

1. When cupcakes are cool, frost them to your liking and garnish with chunks of brown sugar cube.

CAKE

1	egg
⅓ cup (75 g)	sour cream
1 cup (125 g)	all-purpose flour
1 cup (200 g)	sugar
¾ teaspoon	baking soda
⅓ cup (45 g)	graham crackers
½ teaspoon	salt
6½ tablespoons (100 g)	water
⅓ cup (80 g)	Branca Menta*
1 stick (115 g)	butter, unsalted

FILLING

1 cup (230 g)	mint-infused jelly (see Infused Jelly, page 48)
¼ cup (60 g)	bourbon

FROSTING

1 stick (115 g)	butter, unsalted
1 pound	confectioners' sugar
⅓ cup (80 g)	bourbon

GARNISH

fried mint leaf (see Mojito, page 87)

*Branca Menta is one of our favorite lesser-known spirits and is made by the company that produces Fernet-Branca (page 143). It is exceedingly minty and refreshing. You should buy a bottle just to play around with during post-work cocktail hour.

MINT JULEP

For bonus points, bake each cupcake in a silver liner to mimic the iconic silver cup of the Kentucky Derby.

TO MAKE THE CAKE

1. Preheat the oven to 325°F. Line mini cupcake tins with paper liners.
2. In the bowl of an electric mixer, beat egg and sour cream.
3. In another bowl, combine flour, sugar, baking soda, ground graham crackers, and salt. Set aside.
4. Combine water, Branca Menta, and butter in a saucepan and heat until the butter melts.
5. With the mixer on low speed, slowly pour the hot butter mixture into the mixer bowl containing the egg/sour cream mixture. Beat until incorporated.
6. Slowly add the dry ingredients to the wet ingredients and beat until incorporated.
7. Fill cupcake tins two-thirds full.
8. Bake for 10 minutes. Let cupcakes cool completely on a wire rack before filling or frosting.

TO MAKE THE FILLING

1. Whisk the mint-infused jelly until smooth.
2. Add bourbon 1 tablespoon at a time, stirring thoroughly after each addition.
3. Transfer the mint jelly/bourbon mixture to a squeeze bottle.

TO MAKE THE FROSTING

1. With an electric mixer, beat butter with the paddle attachment until fluffy.
2. With the mixer on low speed, slowly add confectioners' sugar until combined.
3. Slowly stream in bourbon and beat until smooth and fluffy, with no lumps or air bubbles.
4. Transfer the frosting to a piping bag.

TO MAKE THE GARNISH

1. Line a plate or sheet pan with paper towels. Set aside.

2. In a medium saucepan, add canola oil halfway up the pan.

3. Heat the oil to 350°F, using a candy thermometer to check the temperature.

4. Gently fry mint leaves* until translucent, about 7 seconds.

5. Remove leaves from the oil and let drain on paper towels. Immediately sprinkle granulated sugar on the hot leaves.

ASSEMBLY

1. When cupcakes are cool, core each cupcake with a small pastry tip. If you don't have a pastry tip, poke a hole in the middle of the cupcake with a narrow-bladed knife (a steak knife will do).

2. Fill the cavity with the mint-infused jelly/bourbon mixture, taking care not to let it overflow.

3. Frost cupcakes to your liking.

4. Garnish with a fried mint leaf.

> *Somewhere in every restaurant kitchen, there are 19-year-old kids picking herbs in an attempt to kick-start a career in the food industry. The many hours spent ruffling through mounds of parsley or mint for only the perfect leaves allows them to contemplate life and the decisions that led to this moment. Eventually, they realize they are only making $7 per hour, and for many this moment of clarity often turns into a career change. This is how waiters are made. For those that stick it out, years after leaving the kitchen, picking herbs conjures up memories of a simpler time, much like remembering the '90s. Give Brooke a list of culinary tasks in the kitchen, and her favorite one will always be picking herbs . . . still for $7 per hour.

SEELBACH

Like all things bourbon from Kentucky, this cocktail has major street cred. Named after the Louisville hotel where it was invented in 1917 (and where Al Capone used to traffic liquor via secret stairways), this cocktail is another example of the fabulous Prohibition tradition of classily spiking champagne with other liquors.

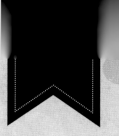

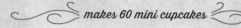
makes 60 mini cupcakes

CAKE

1²⁄₃ cups (208 g)	all-purpose flour
1¹⁄₂ teaspoons	baking powder
¹⁄₂ teaspoon	baking soda
¹⁄₄ teaspoon	salt
1 cup (240 g)	yogurt
¹⁄₃ cup (70 g)	olive oil
1 cup (200 g)	granulated sugar
¹⁄₄ cup (60 g)	lemon juice
2 teaspoons	lemon zest
2	eggs

FILLING

1 cup (230 g)	Sparkling Wine Jelly (page 42)
¹⁄₄ cup (60 g)	Champagne or other sparkling wine

FROSTING

¹⁄₂ cup (115 g)	shortening
1 pound	confectioners' sugar
¹⁄₃ cup (80 g)	bourbon
6 healthy dashes	Peychaud's bitters

TO MAKE THE CAKE

1. Preheat the oven to 325°F. Line mini cupcake tins with paper liners.
2. Place flour, baking powder, baking soda, and salt in a separate bowl and combine. Set aside.
3. Combine yogurt, olive oil, sugar, lemon juice, and lemon zest in the mixing bowl of a stand mixer and beat until incorporated.
4. With the mixer running, add eggs one at a time.
5. With the mixer on low speed, slowly add the dry ingredients to the wet ingredients in the mixing bowl.
6. Mix until just combined, taking care not to overbeat.
7. Fill cupcake tins to the halfway point.
8. Bake for 10 minutes. Let cupcakes cool completely on a wire rack before filling or frosting.

TO MAKE THE FILLING

1. Whisk the Sparkling Wine Jelly until smooth.
2. Add in sparkling wine 1 tablespoon at a time, stirring thoroughly between additions.
3. Transfer the Sparkling Wine Jelly/sparkling wine mixture to a squeeze bottle.

TO MAKE THE FROSTING

1. With an electric mixer, beat shortening with the paddle attachment until fluffy.

2. With the mixer on low speed, add confectioners' sugar.

3. Slowly stream in bourbon and bitters and beat until smooth and fluffy, with no lumps or air bubbles.

4. Transfer the frosting to a piping bag.

ASSEMBLY

1. When cupcakes are cool, core each cupcake with a small pastry tip. If you don't have a pastry tip, poke a hole in the middle of the cupcake with a narrow-bladed knife (a steak knife will do).

2. Fill each cupcake with the Sparkling Wine Jelly/sparkling wine mixture, taking care not to let it overflow.

3. Frost cupcakes to your liking.

MARTINEZ

As the predecessor of the Martini, the Martinez has been sadly forgotten from many a cocktail tale. It is rumored that the Martinez was created in the 1880s to help mask the taste of terrible bootleg gin. The flavors are intense but classic, and it is most recommended for those who enjoy dry, bitter cocktails. While a high-end gin is not necessary for this cupcake, we do suggest that you at least use a gin that comes in a glass bottle. You know, to keep it classy.

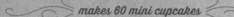

makes 60 mini cupcakes

CAKE

1²/₃ cups (208 g)	all-purpose flour
1¹/₂ teaspoons	baking powder
¹/₂ teaspoon	baking soda
¹/₄ teaspoon	salt
1 cup (240 g)	plain yogurt
¹/₃ cup (70 g)	olive oil
1 cup (200 g)	granulated sugar
¹/₄ cup (60 g)	lemon juice
2 teaspoons	lemon zest
2	eggs

FILLING

1 cup (230 g)	cherry puree with gin (see Fruit Puree, page 51)
¹/₄ cup (60 g)	gin

FROSTING

¹/₂ cup (115 g)	shortening
1 pound	confectioners' sugar
¹/₃ cup (80 g)	sweet vermouth
4 dashes	orange bitters

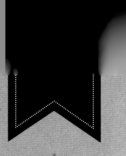

▲
TO MAKE THE CAKE
▼

1. Preheat the oven to 325°F. Line mini cupcake tins with paper liners.

2. Place flour, baking powder, baking soda, and salt in a bowl and combine. Set aside.

3. Combine yogurt, olive oil, sugar, lemon juice, and lemon zest in the mixing bowl of a stand mixer and beat until incorporated.

4. With the mixer running, add eggs one at a time.

5. With the mixer on low speed, slowly add the dry ingredients to the wet ingredients in the mixing bowl.

6. Mix until just combined, taking care not to overbeat.

7. Fill cupcake tins two-thirds full.

8. Bake for 10 minutes. Let cupcakes cool completely on a wire rack before filling or frosting.

▲
TO MAKE THE FILLING
▼

1. Whisk the cherry puree until smooth.

2. Add gin 1 tablespoon at a time, stirring thoroughly after each addition.

3. Transfer the cherry/gin mixture to a squeeze bottle.

TO MAKE THE FROSTING

1. With an electric mixer, beat shortening with the paddle attachment until fluffy.

2. With the mixer on low speed, slowly add confectioners' sugar until combined.

3. Slowly stream in vermouth and bitters and beat until smooth and fluffy, with no lumps or air bubbles.

4. Transfer the frosting to a piping bag.

ASSEMBLY

1. When cupcakes are cool, core each cupcake with a small pastry tip. If you don't have a pastry tip, poke a hole in the middle of the cupcake with a narrow-bladed knife (a steak knife will do).

2. Fill the cavity with the cherry/gin mixture, taking care not to let it overflow.

3. Frost cupcakes to your liking.

NEGRONI

Legend has it, the Negroni was invented in Florence, Italy, in 1919, when Count Camillo Negroni asked that gin be added to his Americano (Campari, Sweet Vermouth, soda), a drink that gained popularity with American expats who remained in Italy after the end of World War I. And thus one of the most iconic cocktails of the twentieth century was born.

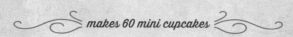

makes 60 mini cupcakes

CAKE

1²/₃ cups (208 g)	all-purpose flour
1¹/₂ teaspoons	baking powder
¹/₂ teaspoon	baking soda
¹/₄ teaspoon	salt
1 cup (240 g)	plain yogurt
¹/₃ cup (70 g)	olive oil
¹/₄ cup (60 g)	lemon juice
1 cup (200 g)	granulated sugar
2 teaspoons	orange zest
2	eggs

FILLING

1 cup (230 g)	orange jelly (see Citrus Jelly, page 45)
¹/₄ cup (60 g)	gin

FROSTING

1¹/₂ cup (115 g)	shortening
1 pound	confectioners' sugar
2¹/₂ tablespoons (40 g)	sweet vermouth
2¹/₂ tablespoon (40 g)	Campari*

---

*The trademark bitterness of the Campari can be overwhelming for some, which is why we suggest cutting the frosting with vermouth. If you, like Leslie, love that bitter Campari flavor, ditch the vermouth and make this frosting with straight Campari.

TO MAKE THE CAKE

1. Preheat the oven to 325°F. Line mini cupcake tins with paper liners.
2. Place flour, baking powder, baking soda, and salt in a bowl and combine. Set aside.
3. Combine yogurt, olive oil, lemon juice, sugar, and orange zest in a mixing bowl and beat until incorporated.
4. With the mixer running, add eggs one at a time.
5. With the mixer running on low speed, slowly add the dry ingredients to the wet ingredients in the mixing bowl.
6. Mix until just combined, taking care not to overbeat.
7. Fill cupcake tins two-thirds full.
8. Bake for 10 minutes. Let cupcakes cool completely on a wire rack before filling or frosting.

TO MAKE THE FILLING

1. Whisk orange jelly until smooth.
2. Add gin 1 tablespoon at a time, stirring thoroughly after each addition.
3. Transfer the orange jelly/gin mixture to a squeeze bottle.

TO MAKE THE FROSTING

1. With an electric mixer, beat shortening with the paddle attachment until fluffy.

2. With the mixer on low speed, slowly add confectioners' sugar until combined.

3. Slowly stream in vermouth and Campari and beat until smooth and fluffy, with no lumps or air bubbles.

4. Transfer the frosting to a piping bag.

ASSEMBLY

1. When cupcakes are cool, core each cupcake with a small pastry tip. If you don't have a pastry tip, poke a hole in the middle of the cupcake with a narrow-bladed knife (a steak knife will do).

2. Fill the cavity with the orange jelly/gin mixture, taking care not to let it overflow.

3. Frost cupcakes to your liking.

makes 60 mini cupcakes

CAKE

1 2/3 cups (208 g)	all-purpose flour
1 1/2 teaspoons	baking powder
1/2 teaspoon	baking soda
1/4 teaspoon	salt
1 cup (240 g)	plain yogurt
1/3 cup (70 g)	olive oil
1 cup (200 g)	granulated sugar
1/4 cup (60 g)	lemon juice
2 teaspoons	lemon zest
2	eggs

FILLING

1 cup (230 g)	raspberry puree with gin (see Fruit Puree, page 51)
1/4 cup (60 g)	gin

FROSTING

2	egg whites
1/2 cup (100 g)	granulated sugar
1/2 teaspoon	cream of tartar

GARNISH

fresh raspberries

CLOVER CLUB

This cocktail predates Prohibition. Although the name of this classic cocktail conjures up images of smoky jazz clubs (in fact, it was named for Philadelphia's Clover Club), the taste is much lighter and softer than you might expect. As a cupcake, it's downright adorable.

TO MAKE THE CAKE

1. Preheat the oven to 325°F. Line mini cupcake tins with paper liners.

2. Place flour, baking powder, baking soda, and salt in a bowl and combine. Set aside.

3. Combine yogurt, olive oil, sugar, lemon juice, and lemon zest in the mixing bowl of a stand mixer, and beat until incorporated.

4. With the mixer running, add eggs one at a time.

5. With the mixer on low speed, slowly add the dry ingredients to the wet ingredients in the mixing bowl.

6. Mix until just combined, taking care not to overbeat.

7. Fill cupcake tins to the halfway point.

8. Bake for 10 minutes. Let cupcakes cool completely on a wire rack before filling or frosting.

TO MAKE THE FILLING

1. Whisk raspberry puree in a bowl until smooth.

2. Add gin 1 tablespoon at a time, stirring thoroughly in between additions.

3. Transfer the raspberry puree/gin mixture to a squeeze bottle.

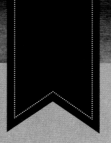

TO MAKE THE FROSTING

1. You'll want to make this frosting once the cupcakes have been filled, as it will begin to lose its fluff with time.

2. In a metal mixing bowl, combine egg whites, sugar, and cream of tartar, and gently heat over a double boiler.

3. Whisk continuously until the mixture is frothy and all the sugar granules have dissolved.

4. Remove from heat and beat with a stand or electric mixer until stiff peaks form—about 10 minutes. (For more on stiff peaks, see "Frosting Techniques," pages 30–31.)

5. Transfer the frosting to a piping bag.

ASSEMBLY

1. When cupcakes are cool, core each cupcake with a small pastry tip. If you don't have a pastry tip, poke a hole in the middle of the cupcake with a narrow-bladed knife (a steak knife will do).

2. Fill the cavity with the raspberry puree/gin mixture, taking care not to let it overflow.

3. Frost each cupcake with a dollop of meringue.

4. Torch each cupcake with a small blowtorch on low setting until the meringue is golden brown. Try not to set the liners on fire.

5. Garnish with a fresh raspberry.

CORPSE
REVIVER #2

Corpse Reviver #1 and #2 fall into that bizarre category
known as "hair of the dog" drinks. We don't know about
you guys, but absinthe and gin don't exactly sound like
hangover treats to us. Pre-hangover, however, this is
a delicious and unique cocktail and cupcake.
And who doesn't like a little absinthe?

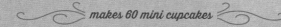 *makes 60 mini cupcakes*

CAKE

1 ⅔ cups (208 g)	all-purpose flour
1½ teaspoons	baking powder
½ teaspoon	baking soda
¼ teaspoon	salt
1 cup (240 g)	plain yogurt
⅓ cup (70 g)	olive oil
1 cup (200 g)	granulated sugar
¼ cup (60 g)	lemon juice
2 teaspoons	lemon zest
2	eggs

FILLING

1 cup (230 g)	orange jelly (see Citrus Jelly, page 45)
¼ cup (60 g)	gin

FROSTING

½ cup (115 g)	shortening
1 pound	confectioners' sugar
¼ cup (60 g)	Lillet Blanc*
4 teaspoons (20 g)	absinthe

GARNISH

orange zest

---

* Lillet Blanc is best known as one-third of the Vesper, the cocktail made famous in Ian Fleming's James Bond novels. In this cupcake, the sugar and absinthe will mask all the subtleties of the Lillet Blanc, so a generic white wine can be used if your local liquor store isn't well stocked with classic French aperitif wines.

TO MAKE THE CAKE

1. Preheat the oven to 325°F. Line mini cupcake tins with paper liners.
2. Place flour, baking powder, baking soda, and salt in a bowl and combine. Set aside.
3. Combine yogurt, olive oil, sugar, lemon juice, and lemon zest in the mixing bowl of a stand mixer, and beat until incorporated.
4. With the mixer running, add eggs one at a time.
5. With the mixer on low speed, slowly add the dry ingredients to the wet ingredients in the mixing bowl.
6. Mix until just combined, taking care not to overbeat.
7. Fill cupcake tins to the halfway point.
8. Bake for 10 minutes. Let cupcakes cool completely on a wire rack before filling or frosting.

TO MAKE THE FILLING

1. Whisk the orange jelly until smooth.
2. Add gin 1 tablespoon at a time, stirring thoroughly after each addition.
3. Transfer the orange jelly/gin mixture to a squeeze bottle.

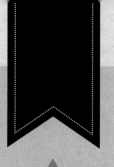

TO MAKE THE FROSTING

1. With an electric mixer, beat the shortening until fluffy.

2. With the mixer on low speed, slowly add confectioners' sugar until combined.

3. Slowly stream in Lillet Blanc and absinthe and beat until smooth and fluffy, with no lumps or air bubbles.

4. Transfer the frosting to a piping bag.

ASSEMBLY

1. When cupcakes are cool, core each cupcake with a small pastry tip. If you don't have a pastry tip, poke a hole in the middle of the cupcake with a narrow-bladed knife (a steak knife will do).

2. Fill the cavity with the orange jelly/gin filling, taking care not to let it overflow.

3. Frost cupcakes to your liking.

4. Garnish with a pinch of orange zest.

BLACKBERRY BRAMBLE

It's incredibly difficult to go wrong with berries, gin, and citrus. Pretty much any combination of the three will lead to a cocktail or cupcake worthy of serving at any gathering.

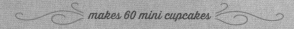
makes 60 mini cupcakes

CAKE

1 ²/₃ cups (208 g)	all-purpose flour
1 ¹/₂ teaspoons	baking powder
¹/₂ teaspoon	baking soda
¹/₄ teaspoon	salt
1 cup (240 g)	plain yogurt
¹/₃ cup (70 g)	olive oil
1 cup (200 g)	granulated sugar
¹/₄ cup (60 g)	lemon juice
2 tablespoons	lemon zest
2	eggs

FILLING

1 cup (230 g)	blackberry puree with gin (see Fruit Puree, page 51)
¹/₄ cup (60 g)	gin

FROSTING

¹/₂ cup (115 g)	shortening
1 pound	confectioners' sugar
¹/₃ cup (80 g)	blackberry/gin juice, reserved from filling (see Fruit Puree, page 51)

GARNISH

lemon zest

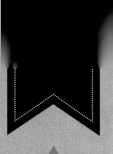

TO MAKE THE CAKE

1. Preheat the oven to 325°F. Line mini cupcake tins with paper liners.

2. Place flour, baking powder, baking soda, and salt in a bowl and combine. Set aside.

3. Combine yogurt, olive oil, sugar, lemon juice, and lemon zest in the mixing bowl of a stand mixer, and beat until incorporated.

4. With the mixer running, add eggs one at a time.

5. With the mixer on low speed, slowly add the dry ingredients to the wet ingredients in the mixing bowl.

6. Mix until just combined, taking care not to overbeat.

7. Fill cupcake tins two-thirds full.

8. Bake for 10 minutes. Let cupcakes cool completely on a wire rack before filling or frosting.

TO MAKE THE FILLING

1. Whisk the blackberry puree until smooth.

2. Add gin 1 tablespoon at a time, stirring thoroughly after each addition.

3. Transfer the blackberry puree/gin mixture to a squeeze bottle.

TO MAKE THE FROSTING

1. With an electric mixer, beat the shortening until fluffy.
2. With the mixer on low speed, slowly add confectioners' sugar until combined.
3. Slowly stream in blackberry juice and beat until smooth and fluffy, with no lumps or air bubbles.
4. Transfer the frosting to a piping bag.

ASSEMBLY

1. When cupcakes are cool, core each cupcake with a small pastry tip. If you don't have a pastry tip, poke a hole in the middle of the cupcake with a narrow-bladed knife (a steak knife will do).
2. Fill the cavity with the blackberry puree/gin mixture, taking care not to let it overflow.
3. Frost cupcakes to your liking.
4. Garnish with a pinch of lemon zest.

SUFFERING BASTARD

As the name suggests, this is a "hair of the dog" drink, intended to get you over a hangover by settling your stomach (ginger), giving you some vitamin C (citrus), and getting you sloppy drunk (gin and bourbon, yikes!). Personally, we prefer a bacon, egg, and cheese sandwich on a roll, but to each his own.

makes 60 mini cupcakes

CAKE

1⅔ cups (208 g)	all-purpose flour
1½ teaspoons	baking powder
½ teaspoon	baking soda
¼ teaspoon	salt
1 cup (240 g)	plain yogurt
⅓ cup (70 g)	olive oil
1 cup (200 g)	granulated sugar
¼ cup (60 g)	lime juice
2 teaspoons	lemon zest
2	eggs

FILLING

1 cup (230 g) cup	Ginger Beer Jelly (page 44)
¼ cup (60 g)	gin

FROSTING

1 stick (115 g)	butter, unsalted
1 pound	confectioners' sugar
⅓ cup (80 g)	bourbon
4 healthy dashes	bitters

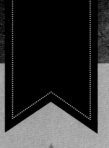

TO MAKE THE CAKE

1. Preheat the oven to 325°F. Line mini cupcake tins with paper liners.

2. Place flour, baking powder, baking soda, and salt in a bowl and combine. Set aside.

3. Combine yogurt, olive oil, sugar, lime juice, and lime zest in the mixing bowl of a stand mixer. Mix on low speed.

4. With the mixer running, add eggs one at a time.

5. With the mixer on low speed, slowly add the dry ingredients to the wet ingredients in the mixing bowl.

6. Mix until just combined, taking care not to overbeat.

7. Fill cupcake tins to the halfway point.

8. Bake for 10 minutes. Let cupcakes cool completely on a wire rack before filling or frosting.

TO MAKE THE FILLING

1. Whisk Ginger Beer Jelly until smooth.

2. Add gin 1 tablespoon at a time, stirring thoroughly after each addition.

3. Transfer the Ginger Beer Jelly/gin mixture to a squeeze bottle.

TO MAKE THE FROSTING

1. With an electric mixer, beat the shortening with the paddle attachment until fluffy.

2. With the mixer on low speed, slowly add confectioners' sugar until combined.

3. Slowly stream in bourbon and bitters and beat until smooth and fluffy, with no lumps or air bubbles.

4. Transfer the frosting to a piping bag.

ASSEMBLY

1. When cupcakes are cool, core each cupcake with a small pastry tip. If you don't have a pastry tip, poke a hole in the middle of the cupcake with a narrow-bladed knife (a steak knife will do).

2. Fill cupcakes with the Ginger Beer Jelly/gin mixture, taking care not to let it overflow.

3. Frost cupcakes to your liking.

PINK LADY

The Pink Lady predates Prohibition, but it wasn't until the quality of gin took a nosedive during the 1920s that this drink really took off. Unfortunately, due to its name and color, it became known as a "girly" drink, but trust us: this drink is way better than your average Cosmo.

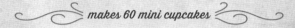
makes 60 mini cupcakes

CAKE

1 ⅔ cups (208 g)	all-purpose flour
1½ teaspoons	baking powder
½ teaspoon	baking soda
¼ teaspoon	salt
1 cup (240 g)	yogurt
⅓ cup (70 g)	olive oil
1 cup (200 g)	granulated sugar
¼ cup (60 g)	lemon juice
2 teaspoons	lemon zest
2	eggs

FILLING

1 cup (230 g) cup	cherry puree made with gin (see Fruit Puree, page 51)
¼ cup (60 g)	gin

FROSTING

2	egg whites
½ cup (100 g)	granulated sugar
¼ teaspoon	cream of tartar

TO MAKE THE CAKE

1. Preheat the oven to 325°F. Line mini cupcake tins with paper liners.

2. Place flour, baking powder, baking soda, and salt in a bowl and combine. Set aside.

3. Combine yogurt, olive oil, sugar, lemon juice, and zest in the mixing bowl of a stand mixer, and mix until incorporated.

4. With the mixer running, add eggs one at a time.

5. With the mixer on low speed, slowly add the dry ingredients to the wet ingredients in the mixing bowl.

6. Mix until just combined, taking care not to overbeat.

7. Fill cupcake tins two-thirds full.

8. Bake for 10 minutes. Let cupcakes cool completely on a wire rack before filling or frosting.

TO MAKE THE FILLING

1. Whisk the cherry puree until smooth.

2. Slowly stir in the gin, adding 1 tablespoon at a time until the desired consistency is reached. Add gin 1 tablespoon at a time, stirring thoroughly after each addition.

3. Transfer the cherry puree/gin mixture to a squeeze bottle.

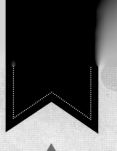

TO MAKE THE FROSTING

1. You'll want to make this frosting once the cupcakes have been filled, as it will begin to lose its fluff with time.

2. In a metal mixing bowl, combine egg whites, sugar, and cream of tartar, and gently heat over a double boiler.

3. Whisk continuously until the mixture is frothy and all the sugar granules have dissolved.

4. Remove from heat and beat with a stand or electric mixer until stiff peaks form—about 10 minutes. (For more on stiff peaks, see "Frosting Techniques," pages 30–31.)

5. Transfer the frosting to a piping bag.

ASSEMBLY

1. When cupcakes are cool, core each cupcake with a small pastry tip. If you don't have a pastry tip, poke a hole in the middle of the cupcake with a narrow-bladed knife (a steak knife will do).

2. Fill the cavity with the cherry puree/gin mixture, taking care not to let it overflow.

3. Frost each cupcake with a dollop of meringue.

4. Torch with small blowtorch on low setting until the meringue is golden brown. Try not to set the liners on fire.*

---

* SPOILER ALERT: You're going to set some liners on fire. Just blow out the flame and serve it anyway. It'll make your cupcakes look rogue and dangerous.

MARGARITA

The Margarita is the most popular and recognizable tequila drink in the United States and has been the fuel for countless table dances and other poor life choices. You can easily make this a flavored margarita by switching out the lime curd for any berry puree (see Fruit Puree, page 51). We suggest adding a little puree to the frosting as well, for taste and a little color.

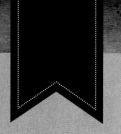

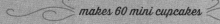

makes 60 mini cupcakes

CAKE

1 2/3 cups (208 g)	all-purpose flour
1 1/2 teaspoons	baking powder
1/2 teaspoon	baking soda
1/4 teaspoon	salt
1 cup (240 g)	yogurt
1/3 cup (70 g)	olive oil
1 cup (200 g)	granulated sugar
1/4 cup (60 g)	lime juice
2 teaspoons	lime zest
2	eggs

FILLING

1 cup (230 g)	lime curd (see Citrus Curd, page 55)
3 tablespoons (40 g)	tequila blanco

FROSTING

1/2 cup (115 g)	shortening
1 pound	confectioners' sugar
1/3 cup (70 g)	tequila
2 teaspoons (10 g)	triple sec

GARNISH

fleur de sel

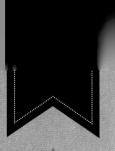

TO MAKE THE CAKE

1. Preheat the oven to 325°F. Line mini cupcake tins with paper liners.

2. Place flour, baking powder, baking soda, and salt in a bowl and combine. Set aside.

3. Combine yogurt, olive oil, sugar, lime juice, and zest in the mixing bowl of a stand mixer, and mix until incorporated.

4. With the mixer running, add eggs one at a time.

5. With the mixer on low speed, slowly add the dry ingredients to the wet ingredients in the mixing bowl.

6. Mix until just combined, taking care not to overbeat.

7. Fill cupcake tins two-thirds full.

8. Bake for 10 minutes. Let cupcakes cool completely on a wire rack before filling or frosting.

TO MAKE THE FILLING

1. Whisk the lime curd until smooth.

2. Add in tequila 1 tablespoon at a time, stirring thoroughly after each addition.

3. Transfer the lime curd/tequila mixture to a squeeze bottle.

TO MAKE THE FROSTING

1. With an electric mixer, beat the shortening with the paddle attachment until fluffy.

2. With the mixer on low speed, slowly add confectioners' sugar until combined.

3. Slowly stream in tequila and triple sec and beat until smooth and fluffy, with no lumps or air bubbles.

4. Transfer the frosting to a piping bag.

ASSEMBLY

1. When cupcakes are cool, core each cupcake with a small pastry tip. If you don't have a pastry tip, poke a hole in the middle of the cupcake with a narrow-bladed knife (a steak knife will do).

2. Fill the cavity with the lime curd/tequila filling, taking care not to let it overflow.

3. Frost cupcakes to your liking.

4. Garnish with just a few flakes of fleur de sel per cupcake.

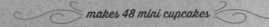

CAKE

1	egg
⅓ cup (75 g) cup	sour cream
1⅓ cups (166 g)	all-purpose flour
1 cup (200 g)	granulated sugar
¾ teaspoon	baking soda
½ teaspoon	salt
½ cup	ginger beer
1 stick	butter, unsalted
⅓ cup (75 g)	minced ginger

FILLING

1 cup (230 g)	Ginger Beer Jelly (page 44)
¼ cup (60 g)	tequila

FROSTING

½ cup (115 g)	shortening
1 pound	confectioners' sugar
2½ tablespoons (40 g)	añejo tequila
2½ tablespoons (40 g)	lime juice

GARNISH

¼ cup	coarse salt
1 teaspoon	cayenne or chili powder

HORNET'S NEST

Developed during a partnership with Hornitos, this spicy cupcake lands high on our list of flavors that have never actually been on our menu. While you could use any añejo tequila in this recipe, Hornitos Black Barrel, a wonderfully rich, almost whiskey-like tequila, adds an unexpected complexity.

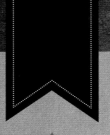

TO MAKE THE CAKE

1. Preheat the oven to 325°F. Line mini cupcake tins with paper liners.

2. In the bowl of an electric mixer, beat egg and sour cream.

3. In another bowl, combine flour, sugar, baking soda, and salt. Set aside.

4. Combine ginger beer and butter in a saucepan and heat until butter melts.

5. Remove from heat. With the mixer running on low, slowly pour the hot ginger beer/butter mixture into the mixing bowl containing the egg/sour cream mixture. Beat until incorporated.

6. Slowly add the dry ingredients to the wet ingredients and beat until incorporated.

7. Add minced ginger and beat until incorporated.

8. Fill cupcake tins two-thirds full.

9. Bake for 10 minutes. Let cupcakes cool completely on a wire rack before filling or frosting.

TO MAKE THE FILLING

1. Whisk the Ginger Beer Jelly in a bowl until smooth.

2. Add tequila 1 tablespoon at a time, stirring thoroughly after each addition.

3. Transfer the Ginger Beer Jelly/tequila mixture to a squeeze bottle.

TO MAKE THE FROSTING

1. With an electric mixer with a paddle attachment, beat the shortening with the paddle attachment until fluffy.

2. With the mixer on low speed, slowly add confectioners' sugar until combined.

3. Slowly stream in añejo tequila and lime juice, and beat until smooth and fluffy, with no lumps or air bubbles.

4. Transfer the frosting to a piping bag.

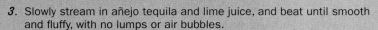

TO MAKE THE GARNISH

1. In a small bowl, combine the salt and cayenne powder. Toss until fully mixed.

ASSEMBLY

1. When cupcakes are cool, core each cupcake with a small pastry tip. If you don't have a pastry tip, poke a hole in the middle of the cupcake with a narrow-bladed knife (a steak knife will do).

2. Fill the cavity with the Ginger Beer Jelly/tequila mixture, taking care not to let it overflow.

3. Frost cupcakes to your liking.

4. Sprinkle with cayenne salt.

TEQUILA SUNRISE

Tequila Sunrise, made popular by Club Med and the movie *Cocktail*, is one of those drinks that you rarely see consumed in the wild. Although relatively tasty and very pretty, it's pretty much a sugar bomb and is probably best enjoyed in cupcake form.

makes 60 mini cupcakes

CAKE

1 ⅔ cups (208 g)	all-purpose flour
1½ teaspoons	baking powder
½ teaspoon	baking soda
¼ teaspoon	salt
1 cup (240 g)	plain yogurt
⅓ cup (70 g)	olive oil
1 cup (200 g)	granulated sugar
¼ cup (60 g)	orange juice
2 teaspoons	orange zest
2	eggs

FILLING

1 cup (230 g)	Cherry Jelly (page 50)
¼ cup (60 g)	reposado or añejo tequila

FROSTING

½ cup (115 g)	shortening
1 pound	confectioners' sugar
¼ cup (60 g)	tequila
2 teaspoons (10 g)	orange juice
teaspoons (10 g)	grenadine

GARNISH

cherry (optional)

TO MAKE THE CAKE

1. Preheat the oven to 325°F. Line mini cupcake tins with paper liners.

2. Place flour, baking powder, baking soda, and salt in a bowl and combine. Set aside.

3. Combine yogurt, olive oil, sugar, orange juice, and orange zest in a mixing bowl and beat until incorporated.

4. With the mixer running, add eggs one at a time.

5. With the mixer on low speed, slowly add the dry ingredients to the wet ingredients in the mixing bowl.

6. Mix until just combined and a few lumps remain. Do not overmix.

7. Fill cupcake tins two-thirds full.

8. Bake for 10 minutes. Let cupcakes cool completely on a wire rack before filling or frosting.

TO MAKE THE FILLING

1. Whisk the Cherry Jelly until smooth.

2. Add tequila 1 tablespoon at a time, stirring thoroughly after each addition.

3. Transfer the Cherry Jelly/tequila mixture to a squeeze bottle.

196

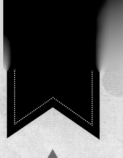

TO MAKE THE FROSTING

1. With an electric mixer, beat shortening until fluffy.

2. With the mixer on low speed, slowly add confectioners' sugar until combined.

3. Slowly stream in tequila, orange juice, and grenadine and beat until smooth and fluffy, with no lumps or air bubbles.

4. Transfer the frosting to a piping bag.

ASSEMBLY

1. When cupcakes are cool, core each cupcake with a mall pastry tip. If you don't have a pastry tip, poke a hole in the middle of the cupcake with a narrow-bladed knife (a steak knife would do).

2. Fill cavity with the Cherry Jelly/tequila mixture, taking care not to let it overflow.

3. Frost cupcakes to your liking.

4. Garnish with a cherry (optional).

BLOOD & SMOKE

We love mezcal.* Mezcal is tequila's badass, cigarette-smoking older sister. It has the same bite and the same syrupy back, but with a delightful smokiness similar to Scotch. It pairs beautifully with a little sweet and a little spicy.

*Mezcal is also extremely versatile, providing a smoky surprise in traditional tequila cocktails and a modern take on many classic Scotch cocktails. Nearly any mezcal will work for the purposes of a mixed drink, but like Scotch, there are a number of high-end mezcals that are perfect for sipping neat.

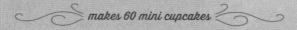
makes 60 mini cupcakes

CAKE

1 ⅔ cups (208 g)	all-purpose flour
1½ teaspoons	baking powder
½ teaspoon	baking soda
¼ teaspoon	salt
1 cup (240 g)	plain yogurt
⅓ cup (70 g)	olive oil
1 cup (200 g)	granulated sugar
¼ cup (60 g)	orange juice
2 teaspoons	orange zest
2	eggs

FILLING

1 cup (230 g)	blood orange jelly (see Citrus Jelly, page 45)
¼ cup (60 g)	mezcal

FROSTING

½ cup (115 g)	shortening
1 pound	confectioners' sugar
2½ tablespoons (40 g)	mezcal
2½ tablespoons (40 g)	blood orange juice

GARNISH

1 tablespoon	coarse kosher salt
¼ teaspoon	dried ancho chile powder
¼ teaspoon	dried cayenne pepper

TO MAKE THE CAKE

1. Preheat the oven to 325°F. Line mini cupcake tins with paper liners.
2. Place flour, baking powder, baking soda, and salt in a bowl and combine. Set aside.
3. Combine yogurt, olive oil, sugar, orange juice, and zest in the mixing bowl of a stand mixer, and beat until incorporated.
4. With the mixer running, add eggs one at a time.
5. With the mixer on low speed, slowly add the dry ingredients to the wet ingredients in the mixing bowl.
6. Mix until just combined, taking care not to overbeat.
7. Fill cupcake tins two-thirds full.
8. Bake for 10 minutes. Let cupcakes cool completely on a wire rack before filling or frosting.

TO MAKE THE FILLING

1. Whisk the blood orange jelly until smooth.
2. Add mezcal 1 tablespoon at a time, stirring thoroughly after each addition.
3. Transfer the blood orange jelly/mezcal mixture to a squeeze bottle.

TO MAKE THE FROSTING

1. With an electric mixer, beat shortening with the paddle attachment until fluffy.
2. With the mixer on low speed, slowly add confectioners' sugar until combined.
3. Slowly stream in mezcal and blood orange juice and beat until smooth and fluffy, with no lumps or air bubbles.
4. Transfer the frosting to a piping bag.

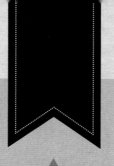

TO MAKE THE GARNISH

1. Combine salt, chile, and pepper in a small bowl.

ASSEMBLY

1. When cupcakes are cool, core each cupcake with a small pastry tip. If you don't have a pastry tip, poke a hole in the middle of the cupcake with a narrow-bladed knife (a steak knife will do).

2. Fill the cavity with the blood orange jelly/mescal mixture, taking care not to let it overflow.

3. Frost cupcakes to your liking.

4. Sprinkle cupcakes with spicy salt.

PALOMA

You'll notice that we don't do much with grapefruit. That's because the distinctive bitterness of grapefruit is easily masked by the sugar used in the cake, frosting, and boozy jam filling—which is why we're going to grapefruit the hell out of this cupcake to make sure the flavor really comes through.

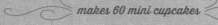
makes 60 mini cupcakes

CAKE

1 ²/₃ cups (208 g)	all-purpose flour
1¹/₂ teaspoons	baking powder
¹/₂ teaspoon	baking soda
¹/₄ teaspoon	salt
1 cup (240 g)	plain yogurt
¹/₃ cup (70 g)	olive oil
1 cup (200 g)	granulated sugar
¹/₄ cup (60 g)	grapefruit juice
2 teaspoons	grapefruit zest
2	eggs

FILLING

1 cup (230 g)	grapefruit jelly (see Citrus Jelly, page 45)
¹/₄ cup (60 g)	añejo tequila

FROSTING

¹/₂ cup (115 g)	shortening
1 pound	confectioners' sugar
¹/₃ cup (80 g)	añejo tequila
2 teaspoons	grapefruit zest

GARNISH

grapefruit zest

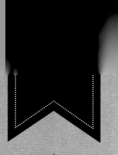

TO MAKE THE CAKE

1. Preheat the oven to 325°F. Line mini cupcake tins with paper liners.

2. Place flour, baking powder, baking soda, and salt in a bowl and combine. Set aside.

3. Combine yogurt, olive oil, sugar, grapefruit juice, and grapefruit zest in the mixing bowl of a stand mixer and beat until combined.

4. With the mixer running, add eggs one at a time.

5. With the mixer on low speed, slowly add the dry ingredients to the wet ingredients in the mixing bowl.

6. Mix until just combined, taking care not to overbeat.

7. Fill cupcake tins to the halfway point.

8. Bake for 10 minutes. Let cupcakes cool completely on a wire rack before filling or frosting.

TO MAKE THE FILLING

1. Whisk grapefruit jelly in a bowl until smooth.

2. Add tequila 1 tablespoon at a time, stirring thoroughly after each addition.

3. Transfer the grapefruit jelly/tequila mixture to a squeeze bottle.

TO MAKE THE FROSTING

1. With an electric mixer, beat shortening with the paddle attachment until fluffy.

2. With the mixer on low speed, slowly add confectioners' sugar until combined.

3. Slowly stream in tequila and beat until smooth and fluffy, with no lumps or air bubbles.

4. Add grapefruit zest, and beat until fully incorporated

5. Transfer the frosting to a piping bag.

ASSEMBLY

1. When cupcakes are cool, core each cupcake with a small pastry tip. If you don't have a pastry tip, poke a hole in the middle of the cupcake with a narrow-bladed knife (a steak knife will do).

2. Fill the cavity with the grapefruit jelly/tequila mixture, taking care not to let it overflow.

3. Frost cupcakes to your liking.

4. Garnish with a pinch of grapefruit zest.

Wine

WHITE SANGRIA

Ah, white sangria—the classy way to get drunk on a Tuesday afternoon, in the middle of summer, with your mom. Everyone has their own variations on the fruit-laden drink, so feel free to experiment to suit your taste. We do recommend using a dry, unoaked white wine, though, as this will already be a very sweet cupcake, and drier wine helps cut the sugar.

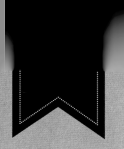

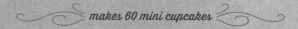
makes 60 mini cupcakes

CAKE

1²⁄₃ cups (208 g)	all-purpose flour
1¹⁄₂ teaspoons	baking powder
¹⁄₂ teaspoon	baking soda
¹⁄₄ teaspoon	salt
1 cup (240 g)	plain yogurt
¹⁄₃ cup (70 g)	olive oil
1 cup (200 g)	granulated sugar
¹⁄₄ cup (60 g)	lemon juice
2 teaspoons	lime zest
2	eggs

FILLING

1 cup (230 g)	White Wine Jelly (page 42)
¹⁄₄ cup (60 g)	white wine

FROSTING

¹⁄₂ cup (115 g)	shortening
1 pound	confectioners' sugar
2¹⁄₂ tablespoons (40 g)	apple brandy
2¹⁄₂ tablespoons (40 g)	ginger beer
1 teaspoon	orange zest

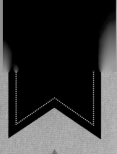

TO MAKE THE CAKE

1. Preheat the oven to 325°F. Line mini cupcake tins with paper liners.
2. Place flour, baking powder, baking soda, and salt in a bowl and combine. Set aside.
3. Combine yogurt, olive oil, sugar, lemon juice, and lime zest in the mixing bowl of a stand mixer, and beat until incorporated.
4. With the mixer running, add eggs one at a time.
5. With the mixer on low speed, slowly add the dry ingredients to the wet ingredients in the mixing bowl.
6. Mix until just combined, taking care not to overbeat.
7. Fill cupcake tins two-thirds full.
8. Bake for 10 minutes. Let cupcakes cool completely on a wire rack before filling or frosting.

TO MAKE THE FILLING

1. Whisk White Wine Jelly until smooth.
2. Add white wine 1 tablespoon at a time, stirring thoroughly after each addition.
3. Transfer the White Wine Jelly/white wine mixture to a squeeze bottle.

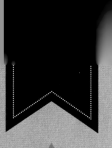

TO MAKE THE FROSTING

1. With an electric mixer, beat shortening with the paddle attachment until fluffy.

2. With the mixer on low speed, slowly add confectioners' sugar until combined.

3. Slowly stream in apple brandy and ginger beer and beat until smooth and fluffy, with no lumps or air bubbles.

4. Add orange zest and beat until smooth and fluffy, with no lumps or air bubbles.

5. Transfer the frosting to a piping bag.

ASSEMBLY

1. When cupcakes are cool, core each cupcake with a small pastry tip. If you don't have a pastry tip, poke a hole in the middle of the cupcake with a narrow-bladed knife (a steak knife will do).

2. Fill the cavity with the White Wine Jelly/white wine mixture, taking care not to let it overflow.

3. Frost cupcakes to your liking.

APEROL
SPRITZ

During our formative years, Leslie was the head bartender at an ill-fated gastropub in Murray Hill. The place went through head chefs like tissues; the worst of them started covertly fixing himself Aperol Spritzes during the middle of his first brunch shift and was so sloshed by the beginning of the dinner shift that he nearly collapsed in the hot kitchen and was fired on the spot. What's the lesson here, boys and girls? Moderation.

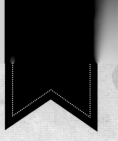

makes 60 mini cupcakes

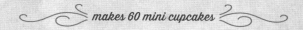

CAKE

1²⁄₃ cups (208 g)	all-purpose flour
1½ teaspoons	baking powder
½ teaspoon	baking soda
¼ teaspoon	salt
1 cup (240 g)	plain yogurt
⅓ cup (70 g)	olive oil
1 cup (200 g)	granulated sugar
¼ cup (60 g)	orange juice
2 teaspoons	orange zest
2	eggs

FILLING

1 cup (230 g)	Sparkling Wine Jelly (page 42)
¼ cup (60 g)	Aperol*

FROSTING

½ cup (115 g)	shortening
1 pound	confectioners' sugar
2½ tablespoons (40 g)	sparkling wine
2½ tablespoons (40 g)	Aperol

---

*Aperol is very similiar to Campari, another rich orange liqueur, without Campari's trademark bitterness. It has a similar flavor to children's nighttime Triaminic, which, if you've ever tried either, you'll know is a compliment.

TO MAKE THE CAKE

1. Preheat the oven to 325°F. Line mini cupcake tins with paper liners.

2. Place flour, baking powder, baking soda, and salt in a bowl. Set aside.

3. Combine yogurt, olive oil, sugar, orange juice, and orange zest in the mixing bowl of a stand mixer and beat until incorporated.

4. With the mixer running, add eggs one at a time.

5. With the mixer on low speed, slowly add the dry ingredients to the wet ingredients in the mixing bowl.

6. Mixing until just combined, taking care not to overbeat.

7. Fill cupcake tins to the halfway point.

8. Bake for 10 minutes. Let cupcakes cool completely on a wire rack before filling or frosting.

TO MAKE THE FILLING

1. Stir Sparkling Wine Jelly until smooth.

2. Add Aperol 1 tablespoon at a time, stirring thoroughly after each addition.

3. Transfer Sparkling Wine Jelly/Aperol mixture to a squeeze bottle.

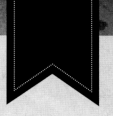

TO MAKE THE FROSTING

1. With an electric mixer, beat shortening with the paddle attachment until fluffy.

2. With the mixer on low speed, slowly add confectioners' sugar until combined.

3. Slowly stream in sparkling wine and Aperol and beat until smooth.

4. Transfer the frosting to a piping bag.

ASSEMBLY

1. When cupcakes are cool, core each cupcake with a small pastry tip. If you don't have a pastry tip, poke a hole in the middle of the cupcake with a narrow-bladed knife (a steak knife will do).

2. Fill the cavity with the Sparkling Wine Jelly/Aperol mixture, taking care not to let it overflow.

3. Frost cupcakes to your liking.

FRENCH 75

You'll notice classic gin cocktails tend to rely heavily on citrus.
The quality of gin in particular was very poor during Prohibition,
so it was almost always served with a heavy dose of citrus
and sugar. Combine those elements or, rather, spike them with
Champagne, and this recipe is the quintessence of Prohibition.

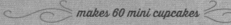

makes 60 mini cupcakes

CAKE

1²/₃ cups (208 g)	all-purpose flour
1¹/₂ teaspoons	baking powder
¹/₂ teaspoon	baking soda
¹/₄ teaspoon	salt
1 cup (240 g)	plain yogurt
¹/₃ cup (70 g)	olive oil
1 cup (200 g)	granulated sugar
¹/₄ cup (60 g)	lemon juice
2 teaspoons	lemon zest
2	eggs

FILLING

1 cup (230 g)	Sparkling Wine Jelly (page 42)
¹/₄ cup (60 g)	gin

FROSTING

¹/₂ cup (115 g)	shortening
1 pound	confectioners' sugar
¹/₃ cup (80 g)	cognac

GARNISH

lemon zest

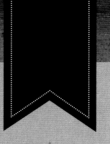

TO MAKE THE CAKE

1. Preheat the oven to 325°F. Line mini cupcake tins with paper liners.
2. Place flour, baking powder, baking soda, and salt in a bowl and combine. Set aside.
3. Combine yogurt, olive oil, sugar, lemon juice, and zest in the mixing bowl of a stand mixer and beat until incorporated.
4. With the mixer running, add eggs one at a time.
5. With the mixer on low speed, slowly add the dry ingredients to the wet ingredients in the mixing bowl.
6. Mix until just combined, taking care not to overbeat.
7. Fill cupcake tins two-thirds full.
8. Bake for 10 minutes. Let cupcakes cool completely on a wire rack before filling or frosting.

TO MAKE THE FILLING

1. Whisk Sparkling Wine Jelly in a bowl until smooth.
2. Add gin 1 tablespoon at a time, stirring thoroughly after each addition.
3. Transfer the Sparkling Wine Jelly/gin mixture to a squeeze bottle.

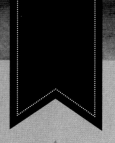

TO MAKE THE FROSTING

1. With an electric mixer, beat shortening with the paddle attachment until fluffy.

2. With the mixer on low speed, slowly add confectioners' sugar until combined.

3. Slowly stream in cognac and beat until smooth.

4. Transfer the frosting to a piping bag.

ASSEMBLY

1. When cupcakes are cool, core each cupcake with a small pastry tip. If you don't have a pastry tip, poke a hole in the middle of the cupcake with a narrow-bladed knife (a steak knife will do).

2. Fill the cavity with the Sparkling Wine Jelly/gin mixture, taking care not to let it overflow.

3. Frost cupcakes to your liking.

4. Garnish with a small pinch of lemon zest.

RED SANGRIA

For those who prefer red wine over white, our Red Sangria has many of the same components as our White Sangria. Pick a mild, slightly fruity red wine like Merlot or Malbec, and stay away from bold reds like Cabernet Sauvignon and Zinfandel.

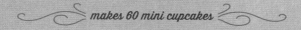

makes 60 mini cupcakes

CAKE

1⅔ cups (208 g)	all-purpose flour
1½ teaspoons	baking powder
½ teaspoon	baking soda
¼ teaspoon	salt
1 cup (240 g)	plain yogurt
⅓ cup (70 g)	olive oil
1 cup (200 g)	granulated sugar
¼ cup (60 g)	orange juice
2 teaspoons	orange zest
2	eggs

FILLING

1 cup (230 g)	Red Wine Jelly (page 49)
¼ cup (60 g)	red wine

FROSTING

½ cup (115 g)	shortening
1 pound	confectioners' sugar
2½ tablespoons (40 g)	red wine
2½ tablespoons (40 g)	pear brandy

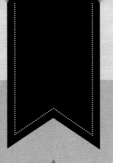

TO MAKE THE CAKE

1. Preheat the oven to 325°F. Line mini cupcake tins with paper liners.

2. Place flour, baking powder, baking soda, and salt in a bowl, and combine. Set aside.

3. Combine yogurt, olive oil, sugar, orange juice, and zest in the mixing bowl of a stand mixer and beat until incorporated.

4. With the mixer running, add eggs one at a time.

5. With the mixer running on low speed, slowly add the dry ingredients to the wet ingredients in the mixing bowl.

6. Mix until just combined, taking care not to overbeat.

7. Fill cupcake tins two-thirds full.

8. Bake for 10 minutes. Let cupcakes cool completely on a wire rack before filling or frosting.

TO MAKE THE FILLING

1. Whisk Red Wine Jelly until smooth.

2. Add red wine 1 tablespoon at a time, stirring thorough after each addition.

3. Transfer the Red Wine Jelly/red wine mixture to a squeeze bottle.

TO MAKE THE FROSTING

1. With an electric mixer, beat shortening with the paddle attachment until fluffy.

2. With the mixer on low speed, slowly add confectioners' sugar until combined.

3. Slowly stream in red wine and pear brandy, and beat until smooth and fluffy, with no lumps or air bubbles.

4. Transfer the frosting to a piping bag.

ASSEMBLY

1. When cupcakes are cool, core each cupcake with a small pastry tip. If you don't have a pastry tip, poke a hole in the middle of the cupcake with a narrow-bladed knife (a steak knife will do).

2. Fill the cavity with the Red Wine Jelly/red wine mixture, taking care not to let it overflow.

3. Frost cupcakes to your liking.

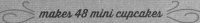

makes 48 mini cupcakes

CAKE

1	egg
⅓ cup (75 g)	sour cream
1 cup (125 g)	all-purpose flour
1 cup (200 g)	sugar
¾ teaspoon	baking soda
½ teaspoon	salt
½ cup (115 g)	stout
1 stick (115 g)	butter, unsalted
⅓ cup (45 g)	dark cocoa powder

FILLING

1 cup (230 g)	Bittersweet Chocolate Ganache, made with ruby port (page 38)

FROSTING

1 stick (115 g)	unsalted butter
1 pound	confectioners' sugar
⅓ cup (80 g)	brewed espresso
½ teaspoon	espresso powder

PORT IN THE STORM

We created this cupcake during our six-month partnership with Divine Chocolate. It is, essentially, everything you would want at the end of a luxurious meal: chocolate, ruby port, and a nice strong espresso. This is an extremely decadent cupcake.

TO MAKE THE CAKE

1. Preheat the oven to 325°F. Line mini cupcake tins with paper liners.
2. In the bowl of an electric mixer, beat egg and sour cream.
3. In another bowl, combine flour, sugar, baking soda, and salt. Set aside.
4. Combine beer and butter in a saucepan and heat until the butter melts.
5. Remove from heat and whisk in cocoa powder.
6. With the mixer running, slowly pour the hot beer/cocoa mixture in the mixing bowl containing the egg/sour cream mixture. Beat until incorporated.
7. Slowly add the dry ingredients to the wet ingredients and beat until incorporated.
8. Fill cupcake tins two-thirds full.
9. Bake for 10 minutes. Let cupcakes cool completely on a wire rack before filling or frosting.

TO MAKE THE FROSTING

1. With an electric mixer, beat butter with the paddle attachment until fluffy.
2. With the mixer on low speed, slowly add confectioners' sugar until combined.
3. Slowly stream in espresso and beat until smooth and fluffy, with no lumps or air bubbles.
4. Add espresso powder and beat until fully incorporated.
5. Transfer the frosting to a piping bag.

1. When cupcakes are cool, core each cupcake with a small pastry tip. If you don't have a pastry tip, poke a hole in the middle of the cupcake with a narrow-bladed knife (a steak knife will do).

2. Fill the cavity with the ruby port Bittersweet Chocolate Ganache, taking care not to let it overflow.

3. Frost cupcakes to your liking.

Wooooooo Bruuuuuuuuuuuunch!

MIMOSA

makes 60 mini cupcakes

CAKE

1 2/3 cups (208 g)	all-purpose flour
1 1/2 teaspoons	baking powder
1/2 teaspoon	baking soda
1/4 teaspoon	salt
1 cup (240 g)	plain yogurt
1/3 cup (70 g)	olive oil
1 cup (200 g)	granulated sugar
1/4 cup (60 g)	orange juice
2 teaspoons	orange zest
2	eggs

FILLING

1 cup (230 g)	Sparkling Wine Jelly (page 42)
1/4 cup (60 g)	sparkling wine

FROSTING

1/2 cup (115 g)	shortening
1 pound	confectioners' sugar
1/3 cup (80 g)	sparkling wine
1 teaspoon	orange zest

TO MAKE THE CAKE

1. Preheat the oven to 325°F. Line mini cupcake tins with paper liners.
2. Place flour, baking powder, baking soda, and salt in a bowl and combine. Set aside.
3. Combine yogurt, olive oil, sugar, orange juice, and zest in a mixing bowl and beat until incorporated.
4. With the mixer running, add eggs one at a time.
5. With the mixer on low speed, slowly add the dry ingredients to the wet ingredients in the mixing bowl.
6. Mix until just combined, taking care not to overbeat.
7. Fill cupcake tins to the halfway point.
8. Bake for 10 minutes. Let cupcakes cool completely on a wire rack before filling or frosting.

TO MAKE THE FILLING

1. Whisk Sparkling Wine Jelly in a bowl until smooth.
2. Add sparkling wine 1 tablespoon at a time, stirring thoroughly after each addition.
3. Transfer the Sparkling Wine Jelly/sparkling wine mixture to a squeeze bottle.

TO MAKE THE FROSTING

1. With an electric mixer, beat shortening with the paddle attachment until fluffy.

2. With the mixer on low speed, slowly add confectioners' sugar until combined.

3. Slowly stream in sparkling wine and beat until smooth and fluffy, with no lumps or air bubbles.

4. Add zest and beat until smooth and fluffy, with no lumps or air bubbles.

5. Transfer the frosting to a piping bag.

ASSEMBLY

1. When cupcakes are cool, core each cupcake with a small pastry tip. If you don't have a pastry tip, poke a hole in the middle of the cupcake with a narrow-bladed knife (a steak knife will do).

2. Fill the cavity with the Sparkling Wine Jelly/sparkling wine mixture, taking care not to let it overflow.

3. Frost cupcakes to your liking.

PEACH SANGRIA

Summer peaches are exceptionally delicious for just a few weeks out of year when you should drop what you're doing and cook everything with a peach. You can barbecue it, boil it, broil it, bake it, and sauté it. You can make kabobs with peaches, and you can pan fry, deep fry, and stir-fry them. There's peach shrimp, peach chicken, peach stuffing, peach jam, peach cobbler, peach salad, peaches 'n' cream, peach sangria . . . that's about it.

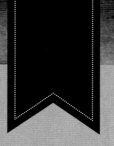

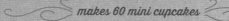 *makes 60 mini cupcakes*

CAKE

1⅔ cups (208 g)	all-purpose flour
1½ teaspoons	baking powder
½ teaspoon	baking soda
¼ teaspoon	salt
1 cup (240 g)	plain yogurt
⅓ cup (70 g)	olive oil
1 cup (200 g)	granulated sugar
¼ cup (60 g)	orange juice
2 teaspoons	orange zest
2	eggs

FILLING

1 cup (230 g)	White Wine Jelly (page 42)
¼ cup (60 g)	peach schnapps

FROSTING

½ cup (115 g)	shortening
1 pound	confectioners' sugar
⅓ cup (80 g)	peach schnapps
1 tablespoon	goji berry powder (optional, for color)

GARNISH

fresh peach*

---

*Keep fresh peaches from browning by tossing them
with a little lemon juice.

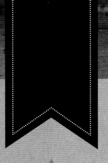

TO MAKE THE CAKE

1. Preheat the oven to 325°F. Line mini cupcake tins with paper liners.

2. Place flour, baking powder, baking soda, and salt in a bowl and combine. Set aside.

3. Combine yogurt, olive oil, sugar, orange juice, and orange zest in the bowl of a stand mixer and beat until incorporated.

4. With the mixer running, add eggs one at a time.

5. With the mixer on low speed, slowly add the dry ingredients to the wet ingredients in the mixing bowl.

6. Mix until just combined, taking care not to overbeat.

7. Fill cupcake tins two-thirds full.

8. Bake for 10 minutes. Let cupcakes cool completely on a wire rack before filling or frosting.

TO MAKE THE FILLING

1. Whisk the White Wine Jelly in a bowl until smooth.

2. Add peach schnapps 1 tablespoon at a time, stirring thoroughly after each addition.

3. Transfer the White Wine Jelly/peach schnapps mixture to a squeeze bottle.

TO MAKE THE FROSTING

1. With an electric mixer, beat shortening until fluffy.

2. With the mixer on low speed, slowly add confectioners' sugar until combined.

3. Slowly stream in peach schnapps and beat until smooth and fluffy, with no lumps or air bubbles.

4. Add goji berry powder (optional) for color.

5. Beat until completely smooth and color is evenly distributed.

6. Transfer the frosting to a piping bag.

ASSEMBLY

1. When cupcakes are cool, core each cupcake with a small pastry tip. If you don't have a pastry tip, poke a hole in the middle of the cupcake with a narrow-bladed knife (a steak knife will do).

2. Fill the cavity with the White Wine Jelly/peach schnapps mixture, taking care not to let it overflow.

3. Frost cupcakes to your liking.

4. Garnish with a fresh peach cube.

Beer / Cider

APPLES TO APPLES

Autumn is quite possibly the best season for baking, largely due to the abundance of delicious apples and the acceptance of gorging on pumpkin anything whenever possible. Combining some of the best things about the season, this cupcake would be perfect for Thanksgiving or Halloween.

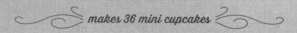

makes 36 mini cupcakes

CAKE

1⅓ cups (166 g)	all-purpose flour
1 cup (200 g)	granulated sugar
½ teaspoon	baking soda
½ teaspoon	salt
1½ teaspoons	cinnamon
2	eggs
1 cup (230 g)	cooked pumpkin
¾ cup (160 g)	canola or safflower oil

FILLING

¼ cup (60 g)	applejack brandy
1 cup (230 g)	Applesauce (page 54)

FROSTING

¼ cup (60 g)	butter
¼ cup (60 g)	cream cheese
1 pound	confectioners' sugar
⅓ cup (80 g)	applejack brandy
½ teaspoon	cinnamon
½ teaspoon	ground cloves

TO MAKE THE CAKE

1. Preheat the oven to 325°F. Line mini cupcake tins with paper liners.
2. Combine flour, sugar, baking soda, salt, and cinnamon in a mixing bowl.
3. Beat eggs in a separate bowl.
4. Create a well in the center of the dry ingredients.
5. Add pumpkin, oil, and eggs.
6. Mix just until smooth.
7. Fill cupcake tins two-thirds full.
8. Bake for 10 minutes. Let cupcakes cool completely on a wire rack before filling or frosting.

TO MAKE THE FILLING

1. Add applejack 1 tablespoon at a time into Applesauce, stirring thoroughly after each addition.
2. Transfer the filling to a squeeze bottle.

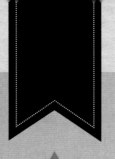

TO MAKE THE FROSTING

1. With an electric mixer, beat butter and cream cheese until combined and fluffy.

2. With the mixer on low speed, slowly add confectioners' sugar until combined.

3. Continuing with the mixer on low speed, slowly stream in the applejack.

4. Add cinnamon and cloves, and beat until smooth and fluffy, with no lumps or air bubbles.

5. Transfer the frosting to a piping bag.

ASSEMBLY

1. When cupcakes are cool, core each cupcake with a small pastry tip. If you don't have a pastry tip, poke a hole in the middle of the cupcake with a narrow-bladed knife (a steak knife will do).

2. Fill the cavity with the Applesauce/applejack mixture, taking care not to let it overflow.

3. Frost cupcakes to your liking.

SAUCY PUMPKIN

During our first fall at Prohibition Bakery, we wanted to create a pumpkin cupcake that was different from all the typical, spiced pumpkin lattes and pastries that bombard us every autumn. By incorporating sage and pumpkin seeds, we imbued the pumpkin cake with earthy flavors and tied it all together with the bitterness of Oktoberfest beer and a hint of chocolate.

CAKE

¾ cup plus 2 tablespoons (110 g)	all-purpose flour
½ teaspoon	baking soda
½ teaspoon	salt
⅛ teaspoon	ground cloves
⅛ teaspoon	cinnamon
⅛ teaspoon	ground nutmeg
½ cup (106 g)	roasted pumpkin puree (store-bought is fine)
1	egg
¼ cup (60 g)	canola oil
¼ cup (60 g)	Oktoberfest beer
½ cup plus 2 tablespoons (125 g)	granulated sugar
½ teaspoon	vanilla

FILLING

1 cup (230 g)	Sage Ganache (page 40)

OKTOBERFEST REDUCTION

2 bottles (24 ounces)	Oktoberfest beer

FROSTING

1 stick (115 g)	butter, unsalted
1 pound	confectioners' sugar
⅓ cup (80 g)	Oktoberfest reduction (see instructions below)
¼ cup	ground hulled pumpkin seeds, toasted

GARNISH

1	quart canola oil
1 bunch	sage leaves
½ teaspoon	salt

TO MAKE THE CAKE

1. Preheat the oven to 325°F. Line mini cupcake tins with paper liners.
2. Place flour, baking soda, salt, cloves, cinnamon, and nutmeg in a bowl and combine. Set aside.
3. Combine pumpkin puree, egg, canola oil, beer, sugar, and vanilla in the mixing bowl of an electric mixer and beat until incorporated.
4. Slowly add the dry ingredients to the wet ingredients and beat until smooth.
5. Fill cupcake tins two-thirds full.
6. Bake for 10 minutes. Let cupcakes cool completely on a wire rack before filling or frosting.

TO MAKE THE OKTOBERFEST REDUCTION

1. In a large pan, bring beer to a boil and reduce by three-quarters. The liquid will be bitter and slightly syrupy. Take care not to let the beer boil over.
2. Transfer the reduction to a container and let cool completely.

TO MAKE THE FROSTING

1. With an electric mixer, beat butter with the paddle attachment until fluffy.
2. With the mixer on low speed, slowly add confectioners' sugar until combined.
3. Slowly stream in Oktoberfest reduction and beat until smooth and fluffy, with no lumps or air bubbles.
4. Add ground pumpkin seeds and beat until incorporated.
5. Transfer the frosting to a piping bag.

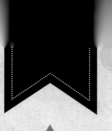

TO MAKE THE GARNISH

1. In a saucepan, heat the canola oil to 325°F.
2. Line a sheet pan or plate with a paper towel, for draining.
3. While the oil is heating, remove sage leaves from stems, rinse, dry, roll, and slice into thin strips, about ¼ inch thick.
4. Carefully fry sage ribbons until bubbling nearly subsides, about 15 seconds.
5. Remove the sage ribbons from the oil with a slotted spoon or strainer and let drain on paper towels.
6. While the sage leaves are still hot, immediately sprinkle them with salt.

ASSEMBLY

1. When cupcakes are cool, core each cupcake with a small pastry tip. If you don't have a pastry tip, poke a hole in the middle of the cupcake with a narrow-bladed knife (a steak knife will do).
2. Fill the cavity with Sage Ganache, taking care not to let it overflow.
3. Frost cupcakes to your liking.
4. Garnish with a fried sage leaf.

CAMPFIRE

This is based upon a cocktail created during late nights at the bakery and leftover bits of this and that (beer, Scotch, and graham crackers). The smoky quality of the Scotch can overpower the more subtle stout, which is why the stout is reinforced in the ganache.

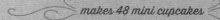

makes 48 mini cupcakes

CAKE

1	egg
⅓ cup (75 g)	sour cream
¾ cup (100 g)	all-purpose flour
⅓ cup (70 g)	ground graham crackers
1 cup (200 g)	granulated sugar
¾ teaspoon	baking soda
½ teaspoon	salt
½ teaspoon	black pepper
½ cup (115 g)	stout
1 stick (115 g)	butter, unsalted

FILLING

1 cup (230 g)	Bittersweet Chocolate Ganache, made with stout (page 38)

FROSTING

1 stick (115 g)	butter, unsalted
1 pound	confectioners' sugar
⅓ cup (80 g)	lightly peated Scotch, such as Talisker

GARNISH

crushed graham crackers

TO MAKE THE CAKE

1. Preheat the oven to 325°F. Line mini cupcake tins with paper liners.

2. In the bowl of an electric mixer, beat egg and sour cream until incorporated.

3. In another bowl, combine flour, ground graham crackers, sugar, baking soda, salt, and pepper. Set aside.

4. Combine stout and butter in a saucepan and heat until the butter melts.

5. Remove from heat. While the mixer is running on low, slowly pour the hot beer/butter mixture into the mixing bowl containing the egg/sour cream mixture. Mix until incorporated.

6. Slowly add the dry ingredients to the wet ingredients and beat until incorporated.

7. Fill cupcake tins two-thirds full.

8. Bake for 10 minutes. Let cupcakes cool completely on a wire rack before filling or frosting.

TO MAKE THE FROSTING

1. With an electric mixer, beat butter with the paddle attachment until fluffy.

2. With the mixer on low speed, slowly add confectioners' sugar until incorporated.

3. Slowly stream in Scotch.

4. Transfer the frosting to a piping bag.

ASSEMBLY

1. When cupcakes are cool, core each cupcake with a small pastry tip. If you don't have a pastry tip, poke a hole in the middle of the cupcake with a narrow-bladed knife (a steak knife will do).

2. Fill the cavity with stout Bittersweet Chocolate Ganache, taking care not to let it overflow.

3. Frost cupcakes to your liking.

4. Garnish with crushed graham crackers.

JOHNNY APPLESEED'S DIRTY LITTLE SECRET

While hard cider has been around since the days of yore, it seems that it has been accepted only recently into the world of beer, wine, and spirits. We're going to go ahead and assume that Johnny Appleseed's legendary kindness and conversation wasn't just due to an apple-laden diet of vitamins and minerals, and that he was likely distilling his own happiness while on the road. The man was using a cooking pot as a hat, after all.

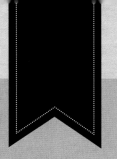

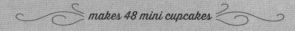

makes 48 mini cupcakes

CAKE

1	egg
⅓ cup (75 g)	sour cream
1⅓ cup (166 g)	all-purpose flour
1 cup (200 g)	granulated sugar
¾ teaspoon	baking soda
1 teaspoon	lemon zest
1 teaspoon	cinnamon
½ teaspoon	nutmeg
½ teaspoon	salt
½ cup (115 g)	tart hard cider*
1 stick (115 g)	butter, unsalted

FILLING

1 cup (230 g)	Hard Cider Jelly (page 46)

FROSTING

1 stick (115 g)	butter, unsalted, or ½ cup plus 1 tablespoon shortening
1 pound	confectioners' sugar
¼ teaspoon	cinnamon
⅓ cup (80 g)	tart hard cider*

GARNISH

1 green apple
1 lemon

---

*Go with the tartest cider you can find. We like McKenzie's Green Apple.

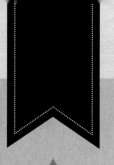

TO MAKE THE CAKE

1. Preheat the oven to 325°F. Line mini cupcake tins with paper liners.
2. In the bowl of an electric mixer, beat egg and sour cream until incorporated.
3. In another bowl, combine flour, sugar, baking soda, lemon zest, cinnamon, nutmeg, and salt. Set aside.
4. Combine hard cider and butter in a saucepan and heat until butter melts.
5. Remove from heat. While the mixer is running, slowly stream in the hot butter/cider mixture.
6. Slowly add the dry ingredients to the wet ingredients and beat until incorporated.
7. Fill cupcake tins two-thirds full.
8. Bake for 10 minutes. Let cupcakes cool completely on a wire rack before filling or frosting.

TO MAKE THE FROSTING

1. With an electric mixer, beat butter with the paddle attachment until fluffy.
2. With the mixer on low speed, slowly add confectioners' sugar and cinnamon until incorporated.
3. Slowly stream in cider and beat until smooth and fluffy, with no lumps or air bubbles.
4. Transfer the frosting to a piping bag.

TO MAKE THE GARNISH

1. Brunoise* the apple slices.

2. Squeeze lemon juice over the brunoise to keep the apples from browning.

ASSEMBLY

1. When cupcakes are cool, core each cupcake with a small pastry tip. If you don't have a pastry tip, poke a hole in the middle of the cupcake with a narrow-bladed knife (a steak knife will do).

2. Fill the cavity with the Hard Cider Jelly, taking care not to let it overflow.

3. Frost cupcakes to your liking.

4. Let the apple brunoise drain on a paper towel, and garnish each cupcake with a few tiny cubes.

---

*Brunoise is simply a fancy French term for using a knife to make a teeny tiny little dice, about ⅛ inch cubes. Yes, we know that sounds fussy and time-consuming . . . and it is . . . but it also looks adorable and is a great way to fool people into thinking you're a master baker.

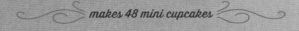
CAKE

1	egg
⅓ cup (75 g)	sour cream
1⅓ cup (166 g)	all-purpose flour
1 cup (200 g)	granulated sugar
¾ teaspoon	baking soda
½ teaspoon	salt
1 teaspoon	lemon zest
½ teaspoon	coriander
½ teaspoon	caraway
½ cup (115 g)	unfiltered wheat ale, such as Southampton Brewery's Publick House Gran Cru Pale Ale
1 stick (115 g)	butter, unsalted

FILLING

1 cup (230 g)	Wheat Beer Jelly (page 47)

FROSTING

1 stick (115 g)	butter, unsalted
1 pound	confectioners' sugar
⅓ cup (80 g)	wheat ale
½ teaspoon	coriander
½ teaspoon	caraway
½ teaspoon	orange zest

GARNISH

1 quart	canola oil, for frying
2 tablespoons	sugar
2 tablespoons	salt
¼ pound	purple fingerling potatoes

THE JITNEY

Originally made with Southampton Brewery's Publick House Gran Cru Pale Ale, this springtime cupcake is a sure hit for the beer lovers. The purple potato chip garnish not only adds a touch of color, depth, and texture to this ambitious cupcake, it also enhances the coriander, caraway, and lemon flavors with a subtle hint of salt.

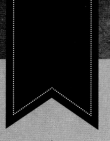

TO MAKE THE CAKE

1. Preheat the oven to 325°F. Line mini cupcake tins with paper liners.

2. In the bowl of an electric mixer, beat egg and sour cream.

3. In another bowl, combine flour, sugar, baking soda, salt, lemon zest, coriander, and caraway. Set aside.

4. Combine ale and butter in a saucepan, and heat until butter melts.

5. Remove from heat. While the mixer is running on low speed, slowly pour the hot butter/beer mixture in the mixing bowl containing the egg/sour cream mixture. Beat until incorporated.

6. Slowly add the dry ingredients to the wet ingredients and beat until incorporated.

7. Fill cupcake tins two-thirds full.

8. Bake for 10 minutes. Let cupcakes cool completely on a wire rack before filling or frosting.

TO MAKE THE FROSTING

1. With an electric mixer, beat butter with the paddle attachment until fluffy.

2. With the mixer on low speed, slowly add confectioners' sugar until incorporated.

3. Slowly stream in ale and beat until smooth and fluffy.

4. Add coriander, caraway, and orange zest and beat until incorporated.

5. Transfer the frosting to a piping bag.

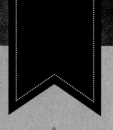

TO MAKE THE GARNISH

1. Preheat oil to 350°F.

2. Combine sugar and salt in a bowl and set aside.

3. Slice purple potatoes with a mandoline, approximately ¹⁄₁₆ inch thick.

4. Gently fry the potatoes until bubbles subside and the potatoes are crispy.

5. Remove from oil and let drain on a paper towel.

6. Sprinkle with the salt/sugar mixture immediately after removing from oil.

ASSEMBLY

1. When cupcakes are cool, core each cupcake with a small pastry tip.
If you don't have a pastry tip, poke a hole in the middle of the cupcake
with a narrow-bladed knife (a steak knife will do).

2. Fill the cavity with Wheat Beer Jelly, taking care not to let it overflow.

3. Frost cupcakes to your liking.

4. Garnish with a potato chip.*

---

* The Jitney has been one of the most popular forms of transportation
to and from the Hamptons since its inception in the late 1940s.
The potato chip on top of this cupcake is our nod to the little
bags of chips passed out on the Hampton Jitney.

TRADITIONAL WINTER WASSAIL

This is seriously old-school, but anyone who's tried this traditional "holiday" punch will tell you it tastes like Santa wrestled Sam Adams in an apple pie, which is to say really, really good. You'll need to make the garnish for this one a day ahead of time.

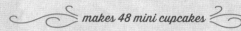
makes 48 mini cupcakes

CAKE

1	egg
⅓ cup (75 g)	sour cream
½ teaspoon	vanilla
1⅓ cup (166 g)	all-purpose flour
1 cup (200 g)	granulated sugar
¾ teaspoon	baking soda
½ teaspoon	salt
½ teaspoon	nutmeg
½ teaspoon	ground cloves
½ teaspoon	cinnamon
½ cup (115 g)	brown ale, such as Bass or Brooklyn Brown
1 stick (115 g)	butter, unsalted

FILLING

1 cup (230 g)	Applesauce (page 54)
¼ cup (60 g)	applejack

FROSTING

1 stick (115 g)	butter, unsalted
1 pound	confectioners' sugar
⅓ cup (80 g)	orange juice
½ teaspoon	cinnamon
½ teaspoon	ground cloves
½ teaspoon	nutmeg
½ teaspoon	ginger

GARNISH

3–4 apples, cored and sliced into ¼ inch thick slices
lemon juice

⅛ teaspoon	cinnamon
⅛ teaspoon	nutmeg
⅛ teaspoon	ground cloves

TO MAKE THE CAKE

1. Preheat the oven to 325°F. Line mini cupcake tins with paper liners.
2. In the bowl of an electric mixer, beat egg, sour cream, and vanilla.
3. In another bowl, combine flour, sugar, baking soda, salt, nutmeg, cloves, and cinnamon. Set aside.
4. Combine brown ale and butter in a saucepan and heat until butter melts.
5. Remove from heat. While the mixer is running on low, slowly pour the hot ale/butter mixture into the mixing bowl. Beat until incorporated.
6. Slowly add the dry ingredients to the wet ingredients and beat until incorporated.
7. Fill cupcake tins two-thirds full.
8. Bake for 10 minutes. Let cupcakes cool completely on a wire rack before filling or frosting.

TO MAKE THE FILLING

1. Whisk Applesauce in a bowl until smooth.
2. Add applejack 1 tablespoon at a time, whisking after each addition.
3. Transfer the Applesauce/applejack mixture to a squeeze bottle.

TO MAKE THE FROSTING

1. With an electric mixer, beat butter with the paddle attachment until fluffy.
2. With the mixer on low speed, slowly add confectioners' sugar until incorporated.
3. Slowly stream in orange juice and beat until smooth and fluffy, with no lumps or air bubbles.
4. Add in cinnamon, cloves, nutmeg, and ginger. Beat until incorporated.
5. Transfer the frosting to a piping bag.

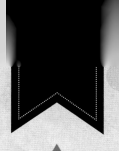

TO MAKE THE GARNISH

1. Twelve to twenty-four hours before you are ready to make the garnish, core 3–4 apples. Slice apples in half with the cores vertical. Then slice the halves into ¼ inch thick slices.

2. Sprinkle the apples with lemon juice to prevent browning, then pat dry with a paper towel or clean dishtowel. Then sprinkle with cinnamon, nutmeg, and clove.

3. Place the apple slices ½ inch apart in food dehydrator* and dehydrate until done, 12–24 hours, or until the apples are brittle, like chips.

4. Store the apple chips in an airtight container. They will keep for up to 6 months if stored properly.

ASSEMBLY

1. When cupcakes are cool, core each cupcake with a small pastry tip. If you don't have a pastry tip, poke a hole in the middle of the cupcake with a narrow-bladed knife (a steak knife will do).

2. Fill the cavity with the applejack/apple brandy and Applesauce mixture, taking care not to let it overflow.

3. Frost cupcakes to your liking.

4. Garnish with apple chips.

---

*If you do not have a food dehydrator, you can dehydrate the apple slices in the oven on baking sheets. Preheat the oven to 150°F and bake apples for 10–20 hours. Rotate the baking sheets every few hours, front to back, top to bottom, and left to right, to ensure even baking. Or, you know, buy some.

PIMM'S CUP

While the Kentucky Derby takes credit for popularizing the Mint Julep, we can thank Wimbledon for launching the iconic Pimm's Cup cocktail into the mainstream. Our Pimm's Cup cupcake was developed after we were approached by Wimbledon to create a special cupcake for the 2013 event, and it turned into one of our favorite (and one of the cutest) cupcakes to date.

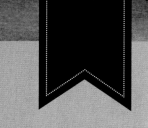

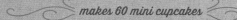
makes 60 mini cupcakes

CAKE

1 2/3 cups (208 g)	all-purpose flour
1 1/2 teaspoons	baking powder
1/2 teaspoon	baking soda
1/4 teaspoon	salt
1 cup (240 g)	plain yogurt
1/3 cup (70 g)	olive oil
1 cup (200 g)	granulated sugar
1/4 cup (60 g)	lemon juice
2 teaspoons	lemon zest
2	eggs

FILLING

1 cup (230 g)	Pimm's jelly (see Liqueur Jelly, page 43)
1/4 cup (60 g)	gin

FROSTING

1 stick (115 g)	shortening
1 pound	confectioners' sugar
1/3 cup (80 g)	Minty Gin (page 34)

GARNISH

1 Persian cucumber, or 1 small English cucumber,
sliced about 1/8 inch thick

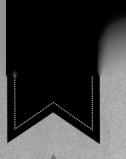

TO MAKE THE CAKE

1. Preheat the oven to 325°F. Line the mini cupcake tins with paper liners.
2. Place flour, baking powder, baking soda, and salt in a separate bowl and combine. Set aside.
3. Combine yogurt, olive oil, sugar, lemon juice, and lemon zest in the mixing bowl of a stand mixer and beat until incorporated.
4. With the mixer on low speed, add eggs one at a time.
5. Continuing with the mixer on low speed, slowly add the dry ingredients to the wet ingredients in the mixing bowl.
6. Mix until just combined, taking care not to overbeat.
7. Fill the cupcake tins two-thirds full.
8. Bake for 10 minutes. Let cupcakes cool completely on a wire rack before filling or frosting.

TO MAKE THE FILLING

1. Whisk Pimm's jelly until smooth.
2. Add gin 1 tablespoon at a time, stirring thoroughly after each addition.
3. Transfer the Pimm's jelly/gin mixture to a squeeze bottle.

TO MAKE THE FROSTING

1. With an electric mixer, beat shortening with the paddle attachment until fluffy.

2. With the mixer on low speed, slowly add confectioners' sugar until combined.

3. Slowly stream in Minty Gin and beat until smooth and fluffy, with no lumps or air bubbles.

4. Transfer the frosting to a piping bag.

ASSEMBLY

1. When cupcakes are cool, core each cupcake with a small pastry tip. If you don't have a pastry tip, poke a hole in the middle of the cupcake with a narrow-bladed knife (a steak knife will do).

2. Fill the cavity with the Pimm's jelly/gin mixture, taking care not to let it overflow.

3. Frost cupcakes to your liking.

4. Garnish with sliced cucumber.

GRASSHOPPER

We're pretty sure no one has ever actually consumed a grasshopper in cocktail form, or that it's even appropriate to refer to a drink that is made from two sugary, low-proof liqueurs as a "cocktail." Either way, it's chocolate and mint, which is pretty much the best dessert combination since booze and cupcake.

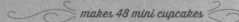

makes 48 mini cupcakes

CAKE

1	egg
⅓ cup (75 g)	sour cream
1⅓ cups (166 g)	all-purpose flour
1 cup (200 g)	granulated sugar
¾ teaspoon	baking soda
½ teaspoon	salt
½ cup (115 g)	stout
1 stick (115 g)	butter, unsalted
⅓ cup (45 g)	dark cocoa powder

FILLING

1 cup (230 g)	Milk Chocolate Ganache, made with crème de cacao (page 38)

FROSTING

1 stick (115 g)	butter, unsalted
1 pound	confectioners' sugar
5 tablespoons (80 g)	crème de menthe*

---

* It's virtually impossible to find clear crème de menthe, so we suggest steering into the skid and serving these up for St. Patrick's Day or . . . Arbor Day?

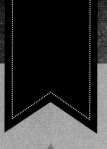

TO MAKE THE CAKE

1. Preheat the oven to 325°F. Line mini cupcake tins with paper liners.

2. In the bowl of an electric mixer, beat egg and sour cream.

3. In another bowl, combine flour, sugar, baking soda, and salt. Set aside.

4. Combine beer and butter in a saucepan and heat until the butter melts.

5. Remove from heat and whisk in cocoa powder.

6. With the mixer running on low speed, slowly pour the beer/butter/cocoa mixture into the mixing bowl containing the egg/sour cream mixture. Beat until incorporated.

7. Slowly add the dry ingredients to the wet ingredients and beat until incorporated.

8. Fill cupcake tins two-thirds full.

9. Bake for 10 minutes. Let cupcakes cool completely on a wire rack before filling or frosting.

TO MAKE THE FROSTING

1. With an electric mixer, beat butter with the paddle attachment until fluffy.

2. With the mixture on low speed, slowly add confectioners' sugar until combined.

3. Slowly stream in crème de menthe.

4. Beat until smooth and fluffy, with no lumps or air bubbles.

5. Transfer the frosting to a piping bag.

ASSEMBLY

1. When cupcakes are cool, core each cupcake with a small pastry tip. If you don't have a pastry tip, poke a hole in the middle of the cupcake with a narrow-bladed knife (a steak knife will do).

2. Fill the cavity with crème de cacao Milk Chocolate Ganache, taking care not to let it overflow.

3. Frost cupcakes to your liking.

4. Using a fine grater, zester, or peeler, garnish cupcakes with milk chocolate shavings.

AMARETTO SOUR

Sweet and sour, this cupcake is great if you aren't fond of a strong, boozy taste or find that one boozy cupcake gets you as tipsy as a co-ed during college orientation.

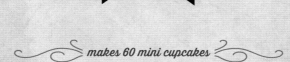

CAKE

1²/₃ cups (208 g)	all-purpose flour
1¹/₂ teaspoons	baking powder
¹/₂ teaspoon	baking soda
¹/₄ teaspoon	salt
1 cup (240 g)	plain yogurt
¹/₃ cup (70 g)	olive oil
1 cup (200 g)	granulated sugar
¹/₄ cup (60 g)	lemon juice
1 tablespoon	lemon zest
2	eggs

FILLING

1 cup (230 g)	amaretto jelly (see Liqueur Jelly, page 43)
¹/₄ cup (60 g)	amaretto liqueur

FROSTING

2	egg whites
¹/₂ cup (100 g)	granulated sugar
¹/₂ teaspoon	cream of tartar
1 teaspoon	orange zest

TO MAKE THE CAKE

1. Preheat the oven to 325°F. Line mini cupcake tins with paper liners.

2. Place flour, baking powder, baking soda, and salt in a bowl and combine. Set aside.

3. Combine yogurt, olive oil, sugar, lemon juice, and lemon zest in the mixing bowl of a stand mixer, and beat until incorporated.

4. With the mixer running, add eggs one at a time.

5. With the mixer on low speed, slowly add the dry ingredients to the wet ingredients in the mixing bowl.

6. Mix until just combined, taking care not to overbeat.

7. Fill cupcake tins two-thirds full.

8. Bake for 10 minutes. Let cupcakes cool completely on a wire rack before filling or frosting.

TO MAKE THE FILLING

1. Whisk amaretto jelly in a bowl until smooth.

2. Add amaretto 1 tablespoon at a time, stirring thoroughly after each addition.

3. Transfer amaretto jelly/amaretto mixture to a squeeze bottle.

TO MAKE THE FROSTING

1. In a metal mixing bowl, combine egg whites, sugar, and cream of tartar, and gently heat over a double boiler.

2. Whisk continuously until the mixture is frothy and all the sugar granules have dissolved.

3. Remove the mixture from heat and beat with a stand mixer or electric mixer, until stiff peaks form—about 10 minutes.

4. Add orange zest.

5. Transfer the frosting to a piping bag.

ASSEMBLY

1. When cupcakes are cool, core each cupcake with a small pastry tip. If you don't have a pastry tip, poke a hole in the middle of the cupcake with a narrow-bladed knife (a steak knife will do).

2. Fill the cavity with the amaretto jelly/amaretto mixture, taking care not to let it overflow.

3. Frost cupcakes to your liking.

4. Use a kitchen blowtorch to toast each cupcake until the meringue is golden brown.

CARAMEL APPLE

A childhood favorite begging for booze, this adult take on a caramel apple is basically healthy since we're making it with fruit juice and nuts.

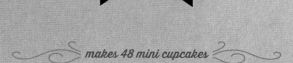

CAKE

1	egg
1/3 cup (75 g)	sour cream
1 1/3 cups (166 g)	all-purpose flour
1 cup (200 g)	granulated sugar
3/4 teaspoon	baking soda
1/2 teaspoon	salt
1/2 teaspoon	cinnamon
1/2 cup (115 g)	apple cider
1 stick (115 g)	butter, unsalted

FILLING

1 cup (230 g)	Caramel Sauce made with applejack (page 53)

FROSTING

1 stick (115 g)	butter, unsalted
1 pound	confectioners' sugar
1/3 cup (80 g)	applejack brandy

GARNISH

1/4 cup (60 g)	crushed almonds

TO MAKE THE CAKE

1. Preheat the oven to 325°F. Line mini cupcake tine with paper liners.

2. In the bowl of an electric mixer, beat egg and sour cream.

3. In another bowl, combine flour, sugar, baking soda, salt, and cinnamon. Set aside.

4. Combine apple cider and butter in a saucepan and heat until butter melts.

5. Remove from heat. While the mixer is running, slowly pour the hot cider/ butter mixture into the mixing bowl. Beat until incorporated.

6. Slowly add the dry ingredients to the wet ingredients and beat until incorporated.

7. Fill cupcake tins two-thirds full.

8. Bake for 10 minutes and let cool on cooling rack.

TO MAKE THE FROSTING

1. With an electric mixer, beat the butter with the paddle attachment until fluffy.

2. With the mixer on low speed, slowly add confectioners' sugar until incorporated.

3. Slowly stream in applejack brandy and beat until smooth and fluffy, with no lumps or air bubbles.

4. Transfer the frosting to a piping bag.

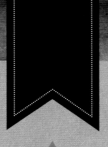

TO MAKE THE GARNISH

1. Preheat the oven to 325°F.

2. Spread the almonds on a sheet pan and toast for 4–5 minutes or until tan in color.

3. Allow almonds to cool and then grind them in a food processer or coffee grinder.

4. Transfer almonds to an airtight container until cupcakes are ready to be garnished.

ASSEMBLY

1. When cupcakes are cool, core each cupcake with a mall pastry tip. If you don't have a pastry tip, poke a hole in the middle of the cupcake with a narrow-bladed knife (a steak knife would do).

2. Fill the cavity with applejack Caramel Sauce, taking care not to let it overflow.

3. Frost to your liking.

4. Sprinkle with crushed almonds.

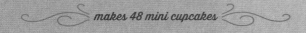

makes 48 mini cupcakes

CAKE

1	egg
⅓ cup (75 g)	sour cream
1 cup (125 g)	all-purpose flour
1 cup (200 g)	granulated sugar
¾ teaspoon	baking soda
1 tablespoon	espresso powder
½ teaspoon	salt
½ cup (115 g)	brewed coffee
1 stick (115 g)	butter, unsalted
⅓ cup (45 g)	dark cocoa powder

FILLING

1 cup (230 g)	White Chocolate Ganache, made with Baileys (page 39)

FROSTING

1 stick (115 g)	butter, unsalted
1 pound	confectioners' sugar
⅓ cup (80 g)	Kahlua

GARNISH

milk chocolate curls

MUDSLIDE

Ah Mudslides . . . the unofficial signature cocktail of Applebee's and Shenanigans the world over. Although they taste like the best Frosty you've ever had, these guys will mess you up if you drink a few. Remember, Kahlua is a rum-based liqueur, Baileys is whiskey-based, and then you add vodka. You're probably better off getting these drinks in cupcake form, unless of course they're two-for-one with your app sampler.

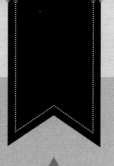

TO MAKE THE CAKE

1. Preheat the oven to 325°F. Line mini cupcake tins with paper liners.
2. In the bowl of an electric mixer, beat egg and sour cream.
3. In another bowl, combine flour, sugar, baking soda, espresso powder, and salt. Set aside.
4. Combine coffee and butter in a saucepan and heat until the butter melts.
5. Remove from heat and whisk in the cocoa powder. With the mixer running on low speed, slowly pour the hot coffee/butter mixture into the mixing bowl with the egg/sour cream mixture. Beat until incorporated.
6. Slowly add the dry ingredients to the wet ingredients and beat until incorporated.
7. Fill cupcake tins two-thirds full.
8. Bake for 10 minutes. Let cupcakes cool completely on a wire rack before filling or frosting.

TO MAKE THE FROSTING

1. With an electric mixer, beat butter with the paddle attachment until fluffy.
2. With the mixture running on low speed, slowly add confectioners' sugar until incorporated.
3. Slowly stream in Kahlua and beat until smooth and fluffy, with no lumps or air bubbles.
4. Transfer the frosting to a piping bag.

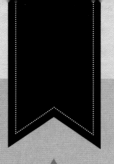

ASSEMBLY

1. When cupcakes are cool, core each cupcake with a small pastry tip. If you don't have a pastry tip, poke a hole in the middle of the cupcake with a narrow-bladed knife (a steak knife will do).

2. Fill the cavity with White Chocolate Ganache made with Baileys, taking care not to let it overflow.

3. Frost cupcakes to your liking.

4. Using a vegetable peeler, garnish with milk chocolate curls.

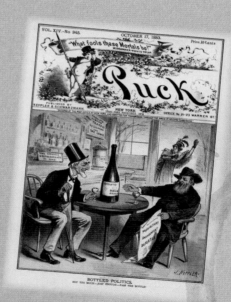

PISCO SOUR

Pisco is a centuries-old, brandy-like liqueur produced in the winemaking regions of Peru and Chile. Both countries claim the Pisco Sour as their national cocktail, which has led to an amusing debate between them. If you've sampled this controversial cocktail, you've most likely had the Peruvian version, with egg whites and bitters, which is also what we're making here.

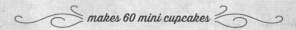

makes 60 mini cupcakes

CAKE

1 2/3 cups (208 g)	all-purpose flour
1 1/2 teaspoons	baking powder
1/2 teaspoon	baking soda
1/4 teaspoon	salt
1 cup (240 g)	plain yogurt
1/3 cup (70 g)	olive oil
1 cup (200 g)	granulated sugar
1/4 cup 60 g)	lime juice
2 teaspoons	lime zest
2	eggs

FILLING

1 cup (230 g)	pisco jelly (see Liqueur Jelly, page 43)
1/4 cup (60 g)	pisco

FROSTING

2	egg whites
1/2 cup (100 g)	granulated sugar
1/2 teaspoon	cream of tartar
1 dash	angostura bitters

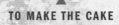

TO MAKE THE CAKE

1. Preheat the oven to 325°F. Line mini cupcake tins with paper liners.
2. Place flour, baking powder, baking soda, and salt in a small bowl and combine. Set aside.
3. Combine yogurt, olive oil, sugar, lime juice, and lime zest in the mixing bowl of a stand mixer and beat until incorporated.
4. With the mixer running, add eggs one at a time.
5. With the mixer on low speed, slowly add the dry ingredients to the wet ingredients in the mixing bowl.
6. Mix until just combined, taking care not to overbeat
7. Fill cupcake tins two-thirds full.
8. Bake for 10 minutes. Let cupcakes cool completely on a wire rack before filling or frosting.

TO MAKE THE FILLING

1. Whisk pisco jelly in a bowl until smooth.
2. Add pisco 1 tablespoon at a time, stirring thoroughly after each addition.
3. Transfer the pisco jelly/pisco mixture to a squeeze bottle.

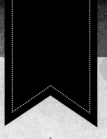

TO MAKE THE FROSTING

1. In a metal mixing bowl, combine egg whites, sugar, and cream of tartar and gently heat over a double boiler.

2. Whisk continuously until the mixture is frothy and all sugar granules have dissolved.

3. Remove from heat and add a dash of bitters.

4. Beat with a stand mixer or electric hand mixer until stiff peaks form—about 10 minutes.

5. Transfer the frosting to a piping bag.

ASSEMBLY

1. When cupcakes are cool, core each cupcake with a small pastry tip. If you don't have a pastry tip, poke a hole in the middle of the cupcake with a narrow-bladed knife (a steak knife will do).

2. Fill the cavity with the pisco jelly/pisco mixture, taking care not to let it overflow.

3. Frost cupcakes to your liking.

4. Use a kitchen blowtorch to toast each cupcake until the meringue turns golden brown.

FLOWER OF OAHU

Sometimes you just wish you could be in Hawaii, particularly when you're sitting in an underground bakery in the middle of a polar vortex in New York City. That's how the cocktail that inspired this cupcake was invented, and that's probably when you should whip up this cupcake.

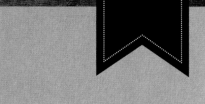

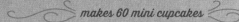 *makes 60 mini cupcakes*

CAKE

1 2/3 cups (208 g)	all-purpose flour
1 1/2 teaspoons	baking powder
1/2 teaspoon	baking soda
1/4 teaspoon	salt
1 cup (240 g)	yogurt
1/3 cup (70 g)	olive oil
1/4 cup (60 g)	pineapple juice
1 cup (200 g)	granulated sugar
1 teaspoon	orange zest
2	eggs

FILLING

1 cup (230 g)	Pineapple Sauce (page 52)
1/3 cup (80 g)	St-Germain*

FROSTING

1/2 cup (115 g)	shortening
1 pound	confectioners' sugar
1/3 cup (80 g)	golden rum

---

* If you're not already familiar with St-Germain, it is a
wonderfully aromatic elderflower liqueur.

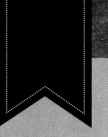

TO MAKE THE CAKE

1. Preheat the oven to 325°F. Line mini cupcake tins with paper liners.
2. Place flour, baking powder, baking soda, and salt in a separate bowl and combine. Set aside.
3. Combine yogurt, olive oil, pineapple juice, sugar, and orange zest in a mixing bowl and beat until incorporated.
4. With the mixer running, add eggs one at a time.
5. With the mixer running on low speed, slowly add the dry ingredients into the wet ingredients in the mixing bowl.
6. Mix until just combined, taking care not to overbeat.
7. Fill cupcake tins two-thirds full.
8. Bake for 10 minutes. Let cupcakes cool completely on a wire rack before filling or frosting.

TO MAKE THE FILLING

1. Whisk Pineapple Sauce in a bowl until smooth.
2. Add St-Germain 1 tablespoon at a time, stirring thoroughly after each addition.
3. Transfer the Pineapple Sauce/St-Germain mixture to a squeeze bottle.

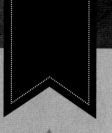

TO MAKE THE FROSTING

1. With an electric mixer, beat shortening with the paddle attachment until fluffy.

2. With the mixer on low speed, slowly add confectioners' sugar until incorporated.

3. Slowly stream in golden rum and beat until smooth and fluffy, with no lumps or air bubbles.

4. Transfer the frosting to a piping bag.

ASSEMBLY

1. When cupcakes are cool, core each cupcake with a small pastry tip. If you don't have a pastry tip, poke a hole in the middle of the cupcake with a narrow-bladed knife (a steak knife will do).

2. Fill the cavity with the Pineapple Sauce/St-Germain mixture, taking care not to let it overflow.

3. Frost cupcakes to your liking.

Building a bar

BOOZE

WITH THIS LIST OF SPIRITS AND WINE, YOU CAN MAKE A
SIGNIFICANT RANGE OF CLASSIC AND POPULAR COCKTAILS:

Vodka, unflavored

White rum

Dark rum

Whiskey (bourbon or rye)

Scotch, peated

Scotch

Tequila

Mezcal

White wine

Red wine

Sparkling wine

Vermouth (sweet and dry)

Bitters—at least two kinds

One fruity/flowery liqueur
(St-Germain, Campari,
Triple Sec, etc.)

One rich liqueur (Kahlúa,
Frangelico, Baileys)

One digestif (Fernet,
Becherovka, etc.)

CREATING A HOME BAR IS ALL ABOUT HAVING SOMETHING TO SUIT EVERY TASTE (MOST IMPORTANT, YOUR OWN), AND HAVING THE TOOLS TO MAKE BASIC COCKTAILS. IF YOU WANT TO START MAKING BERGAMOT TINCTURES, STOCK UP ON EIGHTEENTH-CENTURY POUR SPOUTS, OR CRAFT 30-INGREDIENT FISHBOWL TIKI DRINKS, THAT'S YOUR BUSINESS. THIS IS ABOUT BUILDING A FOUNDATION. WHAT SOME MIGHT CONSIDER A GOOD HOST BAR.

TOOLS OF THE TRADE

These are basic items that come in handy:

- **Jiggers**, ¼ ounce, ½ ounce, ¾ ounce, and 1 ounce—Jiggers, in addition to being a fun word to say, are weird two-sided metal cones that look a little bit like hourglasses. They're used extensively by the pros, but are very easy for a novice to use to get exact measurements. Invest in a few different sizes.

- **Shakers** (2)—Shakers are obviously important for mixing drinks, and they're essential for pretending to be in the movie *Cocktail*.

- **Bar glass**—A bar glass is really just a pint glass. Bar glasses are great for muddling, as they can hold a lot, and you can see how well muddled your mint/cherries/orange/etc. are before continuing to mix your drink.

- **Reamer**—A reamer is great for juicing as you go. Just grab your halved citrus in one hand and ream the juice straight into your shaker.

▶ **Long spoon**—You know, "shaken not stirred"? This is for stirred.

▶ **Zester/channel knife**—While the zester is useful and all, it's really all about the channel knife. This is completely necessary for pretty twists (à la Martini with a twist) and any drink that includes a peel garnish (Old Fashioned, Manhattan, etc.).

▶ **Muddler**—This is that weird thing at a bar that looks like a tiny baseball bat. You use this to mash fruits, herbs, or spices into the bottom of your mixing glass, thereby releasing their aromatics. You'll want to do this before adding any liquid when making Old Fashioneds, Mojitos, Mint Juleps, etc.

▶ **Corkscrew**—Like you don't already know.

▶ **Beer key**—Yes, you can use a bottle opener. But beer keys lie flat in a drawer, are great for opening a lot of bottles quickly (which looks awesome), put less pressure on your thumb, and are super fun to spin around your finger while you pretend to be an old-timey barkeep in the Old West.

▶ **Rocks glass**—This short, squat glass is the receptacle for most of your cocktails.

▶ **Tom Collins glass**—This is a taller, thinner glass that will be used for most of the others.

▶ **Martini glass**—Martini glasses are optional, as you may serve straight-up Martinis, Manhattans, etc. in a rocks glass. However, these drinks look much fancier in a proper Martini glass.

THINGS TO MAKE YOURSELF

The following are recipes for things you can make easily and inexpensively at home. You'll notice that all of the commercial versions of the following recipes for syrups and sour mix have similar ingredients: sugar and fake stuff. Most commercial sour mixes and grenadines are composed of colored and flavored sugar water (or, more likely, corn syrup water). When you make your own much healthier, naturally flavored mixers, you can also adjust the flavors and sugar levels to your preferences and uses, and, of course, it'll impress your appreciative guests.

GRENADINE

Grenadine is probably one of the most recognizable bottles behind any bar, mostly because you've been drinking it since you were a little kid, you big lush, you. What you may not realize is that it's so far from traditional grenadine, it would make Mr. Boston cry. Although the fluorescent pink "cherry" syrup is great for Shirley Temples, real grenadine, which you'll see listed in classic cocktails, is made from pomegranate juice. You can stick to the red dye #5 sugar water if you really want to, or you can whip up some of the good stuff in less time than it would take you to read Shirley Temple's Wikipedia page. Here's how:

1. Add 1 cup pomegranate juice to a medium saucepan over medium heat.
2. Heat until juice begins to bubble around the sides of the pot, but do not allow it to boil.
3. Once bubbles form, remove from the heat, add 1 cup sugar, and stir until the sugar is fully dissolved. This will take a few minutes.
4. Add a couple of drops of orange blossom water and mix thoroughly.
5. Pour into an airtight container. Homemade grenadine will keep up to one month in the refrigerator.

SIMPLE SYRUP

Ohmygodstopbuyingsimplesyrup. Simple syrup is about the easiest thing on earth to make, and is an important part of making a lot of your favorite cocktails (Old Fashioned, Mojito, Margarita, to name a few). You'll find Rich Simple Syrup behind your better cocktail bars, but if all that heating and stirring sounds too arduous for you, or if you're in a pinch and need some cooled simple syrup you can use right now (i.e., if you're working at a busy college bar, or are having some sort of Margarita emergency), you can whip up a quick batch of thinner, less potent Quick Simple Syrup. The difference between Rich Simple Syrup and Quick Simple Syrup is, obviously, that Rich Syrup is twice as sweet per unit of liquid, thereby allowing you to sweeten your drink without diluting it as much as with Quick Simple Syrup. Less water in your booze is, as our good friend Martha would say, "a good thing."

RICH SIMPLE SYRUP

1. Bring 2 parts sugar to 1 part water to a boil in a saucepan while stirring. At first you'll be able to see the grains of sugar; then it will look a little cloudy; then it will be clear when it's ready.

2. Let the mixture cool.

3. Transfer the syrup to a squeeze bottle or other desired container.

4. Okay, you're done.

5. Rich simple syrup is good for up to 6 months when refrigerated.

6. Stop buying simple syrup.

QUICK SIMPLE SYRUP

1. Pour 1 cup each of sugar and room temperature water into a container (at least quart-sized—you want plenty of room) and shake vigorously for 1 minute.

2. Transfer the mixture to squeeze bottle or other desired container. This will likely not dissolve all of the sugar, but it'll get close enough, and the syrup will serve its purpose just fine.

3. Refrigerate. It'll be good for up to 3–4 weeks in the refrigerator.

SOUR MIX

(AKA bar mix, sweet & sour mix)

Here's the thing with sour mix: it's supposed to be sour. I know that sounds obvious, but that crap you see behind most bars, that stuff labeled "sour mix," is basically lemonade—not to imply that it contains any actual lemons, mind you. It's corn syrup with artificial dyes and a pinch of citric acid. But somehow this stuff manages to have the distinction of being both too sour (that weird, fake, Warheads kind of sour) and too sweet (again, corn syrup). We never touch it or put it in anything we make, cupcakes or drinks. Below is the recipe for Leslie's perfect homemade sour mix. Try it in your next Margarita.

⅓ cup (76 g) lemon juice (about 2 ½ lemons)
⅔ cup (144 g) lime juice (about 5 limes)
½ cup (150 g) Rich Simple Syrup

Mix those three things together. Aaaand you're done. Now turn to page 303 and make an awesome Margarita that's not going to make you regret your life choices in the morning.

BLOOD & SMOKE

serves 1

1 tablespoon coarse kosher salt
¼ teaspoon dried ancho chile powder
¼ teaspoon dried cayenne pepper
4–6 standard-sized ice cubes
2 ounces mezcal
1 ounce Solerno blood orange liqueur
½ ounce lime juice*
1 ounce blood orange juice
lime wedge
orange slice (for garnish)

1. Combine kosher salt, ancho chile powder, and cayenne pepper in a small plate or saucer.

2. Fill a shaker with ½ the ice. Add the mezcal and orange liqueur. Add the lime juice and orange juice. Shake vigorously.

3. Run the lime wedge around the rim of the glass. Slowly spin the glass, rim side down, in the salt mixture. Add the remaining ice to the glass.

4. Strain the contents of the shaker into a glass. Garnish with a slice of orange.

*Fresh-squeezed juice is always preferable because it's less likely to have all sorts of additives, it tastes way better, and since you can use the zest in a cupcake recipe anyway, you may as well. Be mindful of seeds.

Cocktails

At this point, the Margarita is really a catchall for any combination of tequila, citrus, and fruited liqueur, and is often thought of as the domain of squealing girls. With the addition of smoky mezcal and spicy salt, the Blood & Smoke is anything but girly. It's the Mae West of Margaritas.

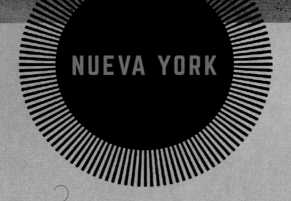

NUEVA YORK

The Manhattan is pretty much the perfect cocktail: It's classic, strong, and spirit-forward, but very drinkable. There is nothing you can do to make it better, but you can still have fun with it, and what's more fun than tequila? Due to smoking and roasting before fermentation and barrel aging, tequila and Scotch share a similar woody, smoky quality that makes them interchangeable in many cocktails—Tequila Old Fashioned anyone?

serves 1

orange peel
Luxardo or dried tart cherry
6 ounces of ice
2 ounces añejo tequila*
1 ounce sweet vermouth
2 dashes angostura bitters

1. Rub the orange peel around the inside and along the edge of the glass.

2. Drop the peel and cherry into the glass.

3. Add ice to a pint glass.

4. Pour in the tequila, vermouth, and bitters.

5. With a bar spoon, stir in a counterclockwise motion for 15 seconds.

6. Strain into the glass.

*You can use mezcal if you want a smokier flavor, but we don't suggest using the less refined reposado or lighter-flavored blanco for this cocktail.

BEST MARGARITA

Leslie makes awesome Margaritas.* She had better, considering that she has prepared tens of thousands of them. Here is her foolproof recipe. Enjoy!

serves 1

¼ ounce fresh lime juice
¼ ounce fresh lemon juice
1 ounce fresh orange juice, retain the peel
2 ounces blanco tequila
1 ounce orange liqueur
½ ounce Rich Simple Syrup (page 298)
kosher salt

1. Combine the juices in a shaker half filled with ice. Keep the squeezed orange; you'll need it in minute.

2. Add tequila, orange liqueur, and Rich Simple Syrup.

3. Shake vigorously for about 15 seconds.

4. Fill a saucer with kosher salt.

5. Run the squeezed orange (pulp side down) around the edge of the glass; then give the glass a little dip in the salt.

6. Fill the glass with ice and strain the contents of the shaker over the ice.

*We view Margaritas as a year-round cocktail and prefer them on the rocks. You can make any Margarita recipe into a frozen margarita—you'll just need a strong blender. Follow this recipe, but instead of straining the drink over fresh ice, just dump the whole thing into a blender.

CAMPFIRE

We tend to get lots of samples of various spirits, beers, edible garnishes, and what have you—and although we can't always find a place for these things on the menu, sometimes we can find a place for them in our bellies. For this recipe, we were gifted with a delicious stout, as well as a bottle of Talisker. Combining the last dregs of each made for a tasty drink.

serves 1

2 ounces lightly peated Scotch, such as Talisker
4 ounces stout
ice

1. Combine the Scotch, stout, and ice in a Tom Collins glass.

2. Drink up.

304

NOT YOUR MOTHER'S COSMO

Thanks to Carrie and the gals on *Sex and the City*, the Cosmo experienced a huge revival in the 1990s. Unfortunately, it flew a little too close to the sun and has since become the symbol of ladies' lunches and book clubs. A real Cosmo is basically a slightly more palatable Martini with the tiniest splash of juice, not the ubiquitous, fluorescent pink that Hollywood's unrealistic standards of cocktail beauty would have you believe.

serves 1

6 ounces ice
2 ounces vodka, mid- to high-end
1/2 ounce triple sec
1/2 ounce pomegranate juice,
or 1 ounce homemade grenadine (page 297)
1/4 ounce grapefruit juice
Twist orange or lemon

1. Add ice to a shaker.
2. Add vodka, triple sec, pomegranate juice, and grapefruit juice, and shake vigorously for at least 15 seconds.
3. Strain into a chilled glass.
4. Add a citrus twist, being sure to twist it over the glass in order to capture the flavorful oils.

A good Bloody Mary is a beautiful thing, but it has so many damn ingredients. The secret is to make a big batch before you go out for the evening, let it come together in the fridge overnight, and then all you have to do is pour it over ice and your booze* of choice in the morning. This is great to make when your college friends come to visit or the in-laws are in town. You'll look like the best grownup ever.

---

*Vodka is the frontrunner, but tequila is great, and there are some weirdos out there that like Ginny Marys.

BATCH BLOODY MARYS

serves 8 Bloody Marys
(3 pints Bloody Mary mix)

FOR THE MIX

4 cups tomato juice*
2 ounces lime juice
2 ounces lemon juice
4 tablespoons horseradish
4 tablespoons Worcestershire sauce
1 teaspoon Tabasco
4 tablespoons Old Bay Seasoning
4 tablespoons black pepper
8 ounces Guinness

FOR EACH DRINK

2 ounces vodka
6 ounces mix

1. Combine all mix ingredients in a large container.
2. Mix thoroughly.
3. Serve immediately or refrigerate for later use.
4. When ready to serve, fill a glass halfway with ice, and add 2 ounces of vodka and 6 ounces of Bloody Mary mix.
5. Garnish to your liking (celery, pickled green beans, bacon, hard boiled egg, chicken wing, grilled cheese sandwich—whatever blows your skirt up).

*If you're using Mr. & Mrs. T, or something like it, you'll want to halve the pepper and lemon/lime juice, as it already has a bit of all three (and a lot of salt).

PEACH SANGRIA

You didn't really think we'd spend so much time talking about sangria and then not teach you how to make some delicious sangria to get white-girl wasted with your friends, did you?

serves 10

2 bottles white wine
$1/2$ cup peach schnapps
$1/2$ cup pear nectar
1 peach, cubed
1 pear, cubed
1 apple, cubed
ice

1. Combine everything but the ice in a large punch bowl.
2. Let the mixture sit for 2–24 hours so that fruit can soak up all the delicious booziness. *
3. Add ice just before serving.

* We all know the boozy fruit at the bottom of the glass is the best part of sangria.

FLOWER OF OAHU

Sometimes we bake late into the wee hours of the morning, and a cocktail or two can really help the hours fly by. We have the benefit of a very well-stocked liquor cabinet, and sometimes Leslie likes to play with the random tidbits left over from various cupcake partnerships and experiments. Thus the Flower of Oahu was born. This recipe can easily be supersized to make a great punch for summer barbecues, or for when you just want to pretend you're on a tropical island.

serves 1

orange wheel for garnish
2 ounces golden rum
1 ounce St-Germain
1 ounce pineapple juice

....

1. Rim a rocks glass with an orange wheel.

2. Add orange wheel to glass and fill with ice.

3. Shake the rum, St-Germain, and pineapple juice together and strain over the ice.

4. Enjoy.

ACKNOWLEDGMENTS

First and foremost, we would like to thank our moms, who, despite getting drunk off of a single Old Fashioned cupcake, have put in countless hours helping us wash dishes or stamp boxes and have spent many a night on the phone telling us that "it's all going to be okay, honey."

To Culture Fix, our 9 Clinton Street Siamese twin: While we don't miss you coming into our space and tearing apart the closet air conditioner at 10 a.m., we certainly miss all the braised meats, after-work beers, and constant stream of ridiculous customer encounters. Clinton Street is figuratively, and literally, less colorful without you.

To Subject LES: Your cocktail wisdom is always appreciated, as is your well-stocked bar.

To Pause Cafe: In addition to keeping us awake with endless cups of coffee, your generous donations of a single orange or knob of ginger have always been appreciated.

To Clinton Street: For letting us be a part of a moment in time in the Lower East Side that will never be re-created.

To all family, friends, current and former flames: Individually, neither of us is exactly easy to put up with. We're not entirely sure how or why you do it, but we're thankful nonetheless.

To Sarah, Ev, Shawn and Rich, Nadin, Stacie, Mike S., Tim D., Stine, Claire, Chrissie, Carly, Jerusha, Amy, and all our Kickstarter backers.

To Tao . . . for reasons and emotions only expressed during Sunday Night Tacos.

To Adam, for putting up with Leslie, even though she never remembers to bring cupcakes home.

To Dolores Bittleman, for keeping Brooke and her puppy sane.

To Jen Cohen, David Goddard, Jennifer Williams, Scott Amerman, Jo Obarowski, Amy Trombat, Chris Bain, Bill Milne, Marilyn Kretzer, Theresa Thompson, and everyone at Sterling for all of their hard work, and for being almost as excited about this book as we are.

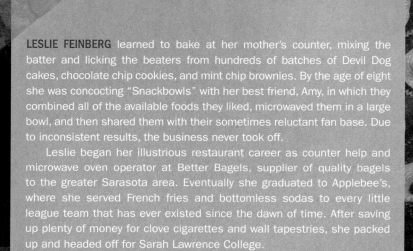

LESLIE FEINBERG learned to bake at her mother's counter, mixing the batter and licking the beaters from hundreds of batches of Devil Dog cakes, chocolate chip cookies, and mint chip brownies. By the age of eight she was concocting "Snackbowls" with her best friend, Amy, in which they combined all of the available foods they liked, microwaved them in a large bowl, and then shared them with their sometimes reluctant fan base. Due to inconsistent results, the business never took off.

Leslie began her illustrious restaurant career as counter help and microwave oven operator at Better Bagels, supplier of quality bagels to the greater Sarasota area. Eventually she graduated to Applebee's, where she served French fries and bottomless sodas to every little league team that has ever existed since the dawn of time. After saving up plenty of money for clove cigarettes and wall tapestries, she packed up and headed off for Sarah Lawrence College.

Upon graduating Leslie made the logical, and not uncommon, transition to waiting tables and bartending while freelancing as an editor and writer for anyone that would have her. She put in time with Alyson Books, Oxford University Press, and *The Onion*, all the while perfecting her Bloody Mary, Jack Daniels oatmeal raisin cookie, and key lime pie recipes.

It was at the height of her quarter-life crisis that she met Brooke and decided to walk away from the glamorous worlds of bartending and publishing and toward the prosperity and stability of small business.

Leslie is most likely to be found at the bakery, covered in confectioners' sugar. She can otherwise be spotted visiting friends in the distant realm

of Queens, investigating vintage cookie recipes, wandering in her backyard (aka Prospect Park) with her boyfriend, or re-reading any one of her favorite books for the umpteenth time. ▲

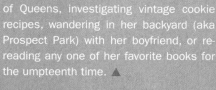

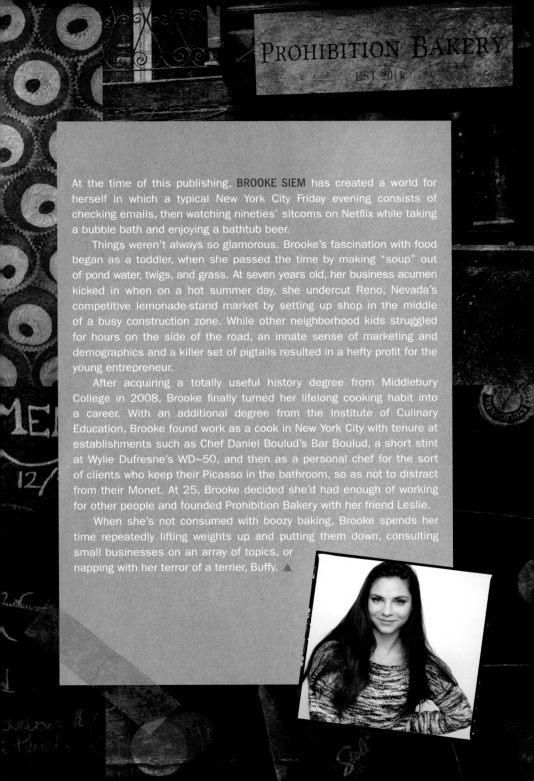

At the time of this publishing, **BROOKE SIEM** has created a world for herself in which a typical New York City Friday evening consists of checking emails, then watching nineties' sitcoms on Netflix while taking a bubble bath and enjoying a bathtub beer.

Things weren't always so glamorous. Brooke's fascination with food began as a toddler, when she passed the time by making "soup" out of pond water, twigs, and grass. At seven years old, her business acumen kicked in when on a hot summer day, she undercut Reno, Nevada's competitive lemonade-stand market by setting up shop in the middle of a busy construction zone. While other neighborhood kids struggled for hours on the side of the road, an innate sense of marketing and demographics and a killer set of pigtails resulted in a hefty profit for the young entrepreneur.

After acquiring a totally useful history degree from Middlebury College in 2008, Brooke finally turned her lifelong cooking habit into a career. With an additional degree from the Institute of Culinary Education, Brooke found work as a cook in New York City with tenure at establishments such as Chef Daniel Boulud's Bar Boulud, a short stint at Wylie Dufresne's WD~50, and then as a personal chef for the sort of clients who keep their Picasso in the bathroom, so as not to distract from their Monet. At 25, Brooke decided she'd had enough of working for other people and founded Prohibition Bakery with her friend Leslie.

When she's not consumed with boozy baking, Brooke spends her time repeatedly lifting weights up and putting them down, consulting small businesses on an array of topics, or napping with her terror of a terrier, Buffy. ▲

PRESS & ACCOLADES

Brooke & Leslie were named as two of Zagat's 30 under 30 in 2014

▼

"Masters of the Art of the Drunken Dessert"
—*Food & Wine, September 20, 2014*

▼

"Just when New York thought it had everything, two lovely ladies opened
the city's first 'Boozy cupcakery' on the Lower East Side."
—*Maxim, November 26, 2013*

▼

"As if anyone could improve upon a good old-fashioned cupcake,
Prohibition Bakery just might have."
—*PureWow, September 11, 2012*

▼

"A room on the Lower East Side whose sole purpose is to create
cupped cakes imbued with plenty of spirited beverage."
—*UrbanDaddy, August 24, 2012*

FEATURED IN:

Wall Street Journal	*Real Simple*
New York Post	*Maxim*
Washington Post	*Business Insider*
Newsweek	*Huffington Post*
Thrillist	*The Today Show*
Urban Daddy	Fox News
Village Voice	NYC Food & Wine Festival
Fingerprints from Condé Nast	*Today with Kathie Lee & Hoda*
Nylon	*MyFoxNY*
Food & Wine	NY1
Playboy	*David Tutera's CELEbrations*
Cosmopolitan	VH1's *Big Morning Buzz*
Town & Country	*Arise and Shine* morning show

Index

Note: Page numbers in *italics* indicate cocktail and cocktail ingredient recipes. All other recipes are cupcake-related.